THINGS YOU KNOW THAT ARE NOT SO

A Digest Of Erroneous Popular Wisdom

DAVID MOSHINSKY

Cover design
by Liz Hutchison

Russet Press
Voorhees, NJ

Things You Know That Are Not So
A Digest of Erroneous Popular Wisdom

By David Moshinsky

Published by: Russet Press
Post Office Box 854
Voorhees, NJ 08043 U. S. A.

First Edition
Copyright © 1995 by David Moshinsky

Publishers's Cataloging in Publication

Moshinsky, David
        Things You Know That Are Not So : A Digest Of Erroneous Popular Wisdom / by David Moshinsky
            p.cm.
            Includes bibliographical references and index.
            ISBN 0-7880-0611-8

        1. Questions and answers. 1. Title.
AG195.m67 1995   031.02

                                QB195-20232

Library of Congress Catalog Card Number: 95-94457

Images copyright New Vision Technologies, Inc.

ISBN: 0-7880-0611-8   PRINTED IN U.S.A

"It ain't so much the things we know that gets us in trouble; it is the things we know that just ain't so."

Artemus Ward

Warning- Disclaimer

This book is designed to provide information in regard to the subject matter covered.. The publisher and author are not engaged in rendering legal, medical or other professional advice. If legal, medical or other professional advice is required, the services of a competent professional should be sought.

The book is written for entertainment and education. It is not intended to be a complete treatise on any subject covered. The author and the publisher shall have neither liability nor responsibility to any person or entity with respect to any loss or damage caused, or alleged to be caused, directly or indirectly by the information contained in this book.

If you do not wish to be bound by the above, you may return this book to the publisher for a full refund.

Special thanks to my family for their encouragement, suggestions and assistance.

Part One

Things You Know About History That Are Not So

What You Know...

Ancient Jews and Israelis are the same people

...that is not so

When the modern state of Israel was born, it took the name Israel, and became a homeland for Jews from all over the world. Considering this and based on common usage for many years, it is natural to assume that the two names, Jews and Israelis always refer to the same people.

However if you use your biblical concordance and look up Jew, you will find that the first place in the Bible that refers to the Jews, the Jews are at war with Israel.

What happened?

To understand the origin of both terms we must go back to Jacob. Jacob had a vision in which God changed his name to Israel, and promised that a great many nations would descend from him.

Later Jacob gave his favorite son, Joseph the coat of many colors. His jealous brothers sold Joseph to an Ishmaelite caravan. The Ishmaelites took Joseph into Egypt. The brothers stained the coat of many colors with blood from a slaughtered goat. They showed their father, Jacob, the coat, and convinced Jacob that Joseph was dead.

When Joseph got to Egypt he became a servant in the house of Potiphar who was captain of the guard for the Pharaoh. There he got the opportunity to interpret the Pharaohs dream and because of the gratitude for his advice became a great and powerful adviser to Pharaoh. Later Joseph forgave his brothers and brought them and their families into Egypt.

The names of the brothers were Reuben, Simeon, Levi, Judah, Issachar, Zebulun, Benjamin, Dan, Naphtali, Gad and Asher. Joseph, himself had two sons, Ephraim and Manasseh.

We now go to the time of Moses. By the time of Moses the descendants of Joseph and his brothers had become slaves. When Moses led these tribes out of captivity, and parted the sea, etc., the tribes called themselves by the names of the brothers of Joseph, and the two sons of Joseph. However all the tribes also called themselves collectively, sons of Israel, or Israel after the name bestowed on their founding father, Jacob.

When they settled in the promised land, each of the tribes occupied a specific area. Some Bibles include maps showing where each tribe lived. In many ways each tribe was like a separate state, with a common central government, just as the fifty United States are separate but under a common federal government. The states of Israel called themselves Judah, Issachar, Zebulun, Benjamin, Dan, Naphtali, Gad, Asher, Reuben, Simeon, Levi, Ephraim and Manasseh.

We can now go to the time of Solomon. Following the death of Solomon, the kingdom split in two. All of the tribes rebelled and formed Israel, except the tribe of Judah. It is the tribe of Judah that was called the Jews. The other tribes called themselves Israel. The first time the Bible speaks of Jews, they are at war with Israel.

The situation can be compared to the rebellion of the United States against the British. The United States were once British subjects. After the war for independence, they no longer called themselves British. Now they called themselves Americans. After the Israelite kingdom split, the two parts were Israel and Judah.

Later the part called Israel went into captivity. They are never mentioned again. They are the lost tribes of Israel. Some

11

scholars believe these Israelites wandered back and rejoined Judah, but other scholars believe they lost any identity and settled in various locations in Europe. Some fanciful stories have them identified as American Indians, or legendary settlers in Ireland (the Tuatha Danaan), or any number of romantic people. One legend has the Stone of Scone as the stone that Jacob used as a pillow when he had his famous dream. This stone lies under the seat that is used by the royal family of Great Britain for coronation ceremonies. The Queen of England was crowned while seated on a stone reputed to be an Israelite sacred treasure. The idea that the British descend from one of the lost tribes is called the British Israelite theory, and has enjoyed great popularity from time to time. All manner of theories abound, but proof is missing.

When the modern state was formed it took the name Israel. Modern Jews frequently refer in their prayers and in their studies to the ancient kingdom that existed before the rebellion. A major part of the Bible relates the history of Israel, concerning itself with the events before the rebellion. After the split both Israel and Judah withered. The name Israel would seem to call back the lost tribes to a new union, and restore the kingdom to a whole. Since no one can be sure which are the missing tribes, this name can only be justified because no other group claims the name. The modern state should more properly be called Judah, as this was the name of the nation that has been restored in modern times.

The identity of Jews with Israel is another example of an error that has grown into fact because it is a universal mistake.

Perhaps even more startling is the strong possibility that few Russian or Polish Jews descend from the Jews of the Bible. The Kingdom of the Khazers has disappeared from common knowledge, but it was once on a par with the Roman Empire and the Arab empire. The Khazars ruled for nearly one thousand years in large portions of the area that later became the Soviet Union. At the height of power, from the seventh through the tenth centuries A.D., The Khazers ruled vast territories inhabited by 30 nations. It

12

is likely that the history of Europe would have been vastly different, if the Khazars had not turned aside the Arab advance in 732 A.D.

The Khakan (Emperor) of the Khazers felt his kingdom should have a modern religion, but the other great empires already had Christianity and Islam. The emperor converted his realm to Judaism. This non-Semitic Jewish kingdom finally broke apart in the thirteenth century, and these Jews formed small pockets throughout the area. There is no way to determine how many Russian, Polish and eastern European Jews are from Khazer and how many from the Diaspora. It is likely that the largest part of the Jews of eastern Europe are descended from the Khazers and not descended from Abraham.

The largest group of Jews that exist today are from eastern Europe. If they are not ethnically part of the "Chosen people" then anti-Semitism becomes a cruel joke on both the haters and the hated.

The modern nation of Israel may have few inhabitants that descend from the tribe of Judah, and as I explained earlier, those from Judah have long ago separated from ancient Israel. Most modern Jews are not only not the same people as ancient Israelis, they are not even the descendants of biblical Jews.

13

What You Know...

Mummies of Pharaohs and great wealth were found in the pyramids

...that is not so.

Most authorities agree that the Pharaohs built the pyramids of Egypt as tombs for themselves. Most authorities agree that the pyramids of Mexico were not built as tombs. Nevertheless no mummy of any Pharaoh was ever found in an Egyptian pyramid. On the other hand many bodies were found in the Pyramid of the Inscriptions at Palanque in Mexico. Others seem to have been sacrificial victims.

The belief that the Egyptian pyramids were built as tombs for the Pharaohs depends on tradition. The tradition goes back thousands of years, but is still open to question. Time after time when the first modern investigators entered the pyramids they reported them looted in antiquity. There is evidence that the pyramids had some funerary function, but it is doubtful they served as tombs for the Pharaohs who had them built.

Two thousand years after the pyramids were built the tradition that the pyramids were tombs for the Pharaohs had become enshrined. Attempts to regain the glory of the old kingdom caused the Egyptians to imitate the ancient practices. Mummies from that later time were interred in one of the pyramids. Peering excavated these in 1837. Later archeologists realized that the mummies were not from the time the pyramid had been built. The entire gallery under the pyramid had been dug out 2000 years after the pyramid had been built.

If the pyramids were not tombs for the Pharaohs, where were the tombs?

The fabulous wealth and the tombs that have been found were found, some in the valley of the kings, and others cut into the rocks at Beni Hasan. The most famous and most fabulous tomb was the tomb of Tutankhamen archeologists found in the valley of the kings.

Because the evidence that the pyramids were tombs for Pharaohs is ambiguous at best, the pyramids have inspired many theories about their purpose. They have been identified as; astronomical observatories, landmarks for interplanetary travelers, mystic power sources, and giant public works projects to keep the masses out of mischief and unite them into one state.

There is something in the human psyche that loves a mystery. The purpose that inspired ancient Egyptians to build these incredible monuments remains obscure, but the common belief, "mummies of Pharaohs and great wealth were found in the pyramids", is something most people know that is not so.

What You Know...

Galileo was tortured by the Inquisition

...that is not so.

The legends about Galileo are replete with misinformation. To start with, the idea that the Inquisition tortured him is completely false. He was a subject of investigation by the Inquisition, and he did recant his position about Copernicus and the Earth moving about the sun. Nevertheless, his treatment was excellent. The inquisitors treated him with respect. He was never held in a dungeon. He stayed as a guest at the Villa Medici, an ambassador's residence, until the actual examination by the inquisition. During the examination he stayed at a five room apartment overlooking the Vatican gardens. He brought his valet, and the Tucson ambassador had his major Domo look after food and wine for Galileo. At no time was he in a prison cell.[1]

After the trial he was sentenced to "formal prison", which turned out to be a luxurious palace in Sienna. A witness said it was a richly furnished apartment. He was also sentenced to repeat once a week seven psalms. Later he returned to his own farm, and still later his own home. The psalms were delegated (with permission) to his daughter who was a nun.

Galileo did not discover sunspots, although he tried to claim priority. Father Scheiner a Jesuit, and his assistant Cystat saw the sunspots and reported them before Galileo. Another man named Johannes Fabricius was the first to publish the news of the discovery of spots on the sun, even before Father Scheiner. Even before any of these, Thomas Harriot in Oxford observed sunspots. He did not publish his discovery until after the others.

Galileo did not invent the telescope, although he did collect a yearly income of 1000 Scudi by presenting the telescope to the authorities in Venice. The first to make a telescope was Johann Lipershay, who showed a telescope at the Frankfurt fair September 1608. Others claimed priority as well, but Galileo certainly does not deserve credit for the invention of the telescope.

Among the most famous things that Galileo did not do, throwing down cannonballs from the tower of Pisa ranks at the top. According to the legend, Galileo gathered members of the University of Pisa, students and townspeople to watch his experiment. Aristotle had declared that heavier bodies fell faster than lighter bodies. The legend attributes to Aristotle the idea that a 100 lb. weight would fall 100 times as fast as a 1 lb. weight. According to the legend, only Galileo disputed Aristotle. Galileo would perform a public experiment to prove Aristotle wrong. In some versions, he put weights of different size into boxes of equal dimension. This would equalize the resistance of the air. In other versions, he merely cast down balls, one of which weighed one hundred times as much as the other. When the onlookers heard the resounding thud of both objects as one sound, science, according to the legend, changed forever. One problem with the legend is that there is absolutely no evidence that Galileo ever performed the experiment.

Coressio, his arch rival, actually did the experiment. Coressio was trying to prove exactly the opposite of that for which Galileo is famed. Coressio was trying to prove Aristotle correct.[2] Aristotle said weights fall faster if heavier, and slower if lighter. Galileo maintained that all bodies fall at the same speed. When Coressio dropped his weights, they did not arrive simultaneously. The heavier weight arrived first. A feather may float, but the effect of air resistance is less obvious when heavy weights are dropped. Coressio was satisfied that he had proven Aristotle correct.

17

Galileo never proved the Copernican system. This would have been impossible, as he had ignored the work of Kepler, and believed in the theory exactly as propounded by Copernicus. These included epicycles, orbits that were perfect circles, uniform speed for the planets, and the sun at dead center. All of these are wrong. Epicycles are little circles on the big circle of the planetary orbit. These artificial motions were needed to adjust the positions of the planets to the observed positions, and to account for the times the planets seem to go backwards in the heavens. Copernicus had the planets moving in perfect circles. The circle seemed the ideologically correct path. Heaven is the domain of God. God is perfect. The circle is perfect. Therefore the planets must move in perfect circles. The reasoning is faultless, but the planets move in elliptical orbits, not circles. Thus the Copernican system did not put the planets at the same places observers did. Furthermore, Copernicus had the planets moving at uniform speed during their entire orbit. They actually move faster when close to the sun, and slow down at the extreme distances. This discrepancy also made the Copernican theory place the planets a long way from observed positions. Finally, Copernicus placed the sun in the exact center of the planetary orbits. The sun is actually at one focus of an elliptical orbit. With all of these errors, Galileo could not possibly prove the truth of the Copernican system. Kepler had long before worked out the correct motion, but Galileo held to the wrong motions described by Copernicus.

Galileo did not work out the laws of inertia. He did much work, and improved human understanding, but the laws were still unknown at his death.

If Galileo never did any of the things on which his fame rests, why is he so important? One reason is that the stories of torture at the hands of the church for the advancement of science make a satisfying tale for bashing of religion. Certain people do not want to give them up, even half a century after they have been proven false. The other is that Galileo founded dynamics as a science.

Galileo formulated the concept of acceleration. His work on changes in velocity and direction caused by the action of force on a body formed the basis of Newton's second law and his great work. When Newton said if he saw further than others it was because he stood on the shoulders of giants, Galileo was certainly one of the giants.

Things You Know

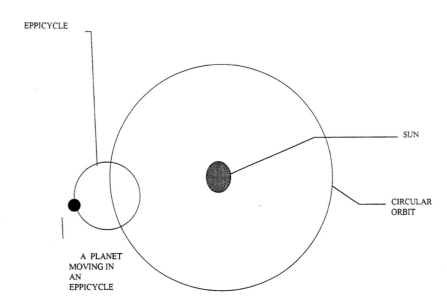

EPPICYCLE

SUN

CIRCULAR ORBIT

A PLANET
MOVING IN
AN
EPPICYCLE

THE COPERNICAN THEORY REQUIRED EPPICYCLES TO PLACE PLANETS AT
PLACES THAT CONFORMED WITH ACTUAL OBSERVATIONS . NOTE THE
DIFFERENCE IN ILLUSTRATION BELOW. PLANETS MOVE CLOSER AND
FURTHER FROM SUN ALONG ELLIPTICAL ORBIT. EPPICYCLES ARE NOT
NEEDED.

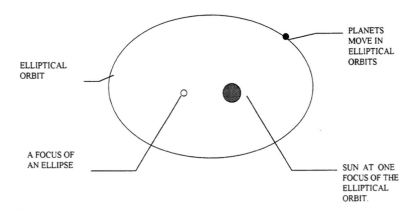

PLANETS
MOVE IN
ELLIPTICAL
ORBITS

ELLIPTICAL
ORBIT

A FOCUS OF
AN ELLIPSE

SUN AT ONE
FOCUS OF THE
ELLIPTICAL
ORBIT.

What You Know...

Edison invented the electric light

...that is not so.

During the cold war, there was a standing joke that the Russians claimed to have invented almost everything of importance. They have a legitimate claim on the electric light. By the time the generator had improved to a point that it could be used for lighting, a Russian, named Lodyguine had erected 200 lights in the St. Petersburg dockyards. The lights had carbons immersed in an inert gas so they burned slowly. These lights created a sensation. Another Russian, named Jablochkoff improved the electric light by using clusters of carbon rods. As one burned up, another automatically moved into place. He also wired them so each was independent. If one burned out the others could continue to burn.

These two Russians produced their lights in 1873 and 1877. Edison produced his light in 1879. Nevertheless, the Russians were not first to produce an electric light. Sir Humphry Davy produced a successful electric light as early as 1808. Sir William Crooks used an electric light in his experiments to produce a variety of strange effects. By 1844, the Paris Opera used arc lights in productions. An American inventor named Charles Brush developed electric lights that were installed in Wanamaker's department store in Philadelphia before Edison made his light.

There were many others who produced working electric lights before Edison. There was even a lighthouse at Dungeness, England that used an electric light as early as 1862.

Why them do we credit Edison with the invention of the electric light? The lights developed before Edison were expensive.They required enormous power. They emitted gases. They were practical only in a large hall or open space. A small light that could be used in a home was needed. That was the improvement patented by Edison. After his improvement, the electric light became usable by people in their homes and businesses.

Edison had developed the electric light by the brute force of trial and error. He had his staff try every alternative they could think of, until a practical filament was found. The development was patented and the patent was very valuable. However, Edison based all his work upon direct current. Today, most electric power is alternating current. The story of alternating current and the human drama that led to the modern world has been forgotten by the public. Today, if you asked the average person who developed our modern system of electric power, some might name Edison, others would name Westinghouse, but very few would remember the authentic genius named Nicola Tesla.

Edison is reputed to have said "genius is 1% inspiration, 99% perspiration". That was true for him, and it was the way most of his inventions were made. It was not true for the man some call America's greatest genius, Nicola Tesla.

Tesla was a child prodigy in his native Croatia. An older brother had been expected to be the family genius, but the brother died in childhood. Tesla felt jealousy over his parents mourning, and determined to be the genius that they had lost. Even as a child he was inventive. At age eleven he developed a crossbow, and sold it to his playmates. When he saw a picture of Niagara Falls, he declared that he would harness the power of the falls for the good of mankind.

He had a long, hard scientific education at the finest schools in the area, and became an electrical engineer. During one class the professor ridiculed Tesla for claiming that he would one day develop an alternating current motor. Tesla did not realize the professor was using ridicule to spur him on. After graduation the professor acknowledged to Tesla that an alternating current motor was his dream too. Tesla promised to contact the teacher when once he had solved the problem of a motor driven by alternating current.

Direct current, the system then used, had limitations that prevented it from the wide use that we now have for electricity. Because of heat loss and resistance direct current can only be carried about a mile. To spread the use of electricity would require a new powerhouse every mile. Furthermore the extra current required overloads the users near the powerhouse, but falls below needed levels at further points. Lights near the powerhouse would burn too brightly and fail too soon. Lights at a distance would be too dim. The cost of so many powerhouses would limit the use of electricity. Direct current was unsuitable for wide distribution, and it actually was harder to produce. Dynamos produce alternating current. A device called a commutater was invented to make the electricity flow out in one direction. The one direction or direct current flow was the only way motors could be powered. No one had figured out how to power a motor with current that flows first one way, and then back the reverse way, over and over.

After graduation, Tesla found employment at the Hungarian government central telegraph office. His work there was rewarded when he was put in charge of the first telephone exchange in that nation. The early telephones were plagued by noise on the line and weak sound transmission. To rectify these problems, Tesla created his first invention, a loudspeaker. This was not patented, but was put into use immediately by the Budapest telephone company.

One day, while strolling in the park, the solution to the alternating current motor came to Tesla like a dream. Tesla had the remarkable ability to envision the motor, and even run it , wear it down, change it, all in his mind. As soon as he was satisfied that the solution would work, he kept his promise to the professor and called him. They had shared the dream of a lifetime, and now must share the triumph.

23

During the next few months Tesla constructed in his mind all the equipment, the dynamos, transformers, and motors that would demonstrate the new system. But he could not get the backing to actually build them. He moved to Paris. There he freely explained his system to anyone who would listen. Another inventor might have feared the invention would be stolen. Tesla did not care, but as it was, he could not give the ideas away. No one was interested, least of all his new employer the continental Edison company.

The company had too much invested in direct current to want any new system. They did, however appreciate Tesla's genius enough to use him as a troubleshooter to handle the most difficult problems. He made all manner of improvements for the company. He was promised a big bonus if he could solve a particularly vexing problem, but after he solved the problem, the bonus was never given. Tesla left France and went to the United States.

Tesla lost most of his money to thieves, and arrived in the United States with four cents and a letter of introduction to the great Mr. Edison. Four cents wasn't even enough for bus fare. Tesla was walking to the room that had been arranged for him when he had a particularly fortuitous encounter. He came across an elderly man in a badly lit little shop, struggling to start a small dynamo. Tesla fixed the dynamo and was rewarded with twenty dollars. Later that man was to prove very important to Tesla.

Edison hired Tesla, but he, too, was not interested in an alternating current motor. When Edison's team of electrical engineers could not repair the electrical equipment on the luxury liner Oregon without taking the ship out of service, Edison sent Tesla to try to save Edison's company from the huge embarrassment and financial loss that would ensue. Tesla was able to do the job quickly and without taking the ship out of service.

When Tesla suggested improvements in the construction and operation of Edison dynamos and motors, Edison told Tesla if they work there would be fifty thousand dollars in it for Tesla. Tesla designed the new dynamos which were patented by the Edison company. They did everything Tesla had promised, but instead of fifty thousand dollars, Edison gave Tesla a ten dollar a week raise. Edison claimed the fifty thousand was only a joke. Tesla quit.

Tesla could not interest investors in his alternating current system, but one group of investors took up an invention Tesla had for an arc lamp for street lighting. A company was formed which prospered, but Tesla did not. The investors got rid of Tesla after they had his invention. Worse yet, to prevent him from suing they spread word that he was fired for incompetence, making it impossible for him to get a job. Tesla had already used his savings for equipment to continue his experiments. Now he was broke and jobless.

He took a job digging a ditch. Times were tough for many that year. Several of the laborers had fallen from successful lives. Hard times had brought them to desperation. Working with him, also digging a ditch was a former stockbroker. They became friends. The stockbroker knew people who could invest in Tesla. After getting Tesla to understand that they could not admit meeting at a common laborer's job, the stockbroker introduced Tesla to an investor. The investor brought in others. One was the man with the broken dynamo that Tesla had repaired on the first day he was in America. He was able to vouch for Tesla's skill. They listened to Tesla explain why alternating current was so superior to direct current. They formed a company with Tesla. Within weeks Tesla completed models of dynamos, motors, transformers, regulators, and every other unit of the power plant. Twenty- five patents were issued in quick succession. The importance, simplicity, and originality stunned electrical engineers everywhere. An epoch making revolution was in progress.

George Westinghouse had the only strong electric company that was independent of Edison. He bought out Tesla for $1,000,000, plus a liberal royalty schedule. After dividing the proceeds with his backers, Tesla had over $400,000. He sent some to his family, some he used to start scholarships at M.I.T, Harvard, and Columbia Universities. The rest he used to finance his experiments. Tesla also continued to assist Westinghouse, to assure that his gift to humanity would get off to a successful start.

Edison tried to destroy Tesla by an interesting subterfuge. He pretended to agree that alternating current was the way of the future. He contracted for rights to use the system. Then he contracted with the state of New York to develop an electric chair for execution of criminals. Edison hoped to destroy the public's confidence in the safety of alternating current. Tesla embarked on a series of public demonstrations to prove the safety of alternating current. Dressed in formal clothes, the tall, elegant Tesla would allow current to pass through his body and light a bulb held in his hand. He delighted in achieving a variety of spectacular effects with electricity passing through his body. By the time his demonstration was over, the audience was enchanted. The safety of alternating current was established.

Success for the Westinghouse company, however, did not lead to financial success for Tesla. Westinghouse was flooded with orders. To grow to meet the demand, Westinghouse turned to banks. The banks refused to lend money. The banks said the royalty promised Tesla was too generous. The company could not meet the growing demand. Tesla wanted to see his work developed with such a passion, that he tore up his contract with Westinghouse.[3] The banks lent the money, and changed the face of America forever.

What You Know...

Marconi invented the radio

...that is not so.

In 1882, Professor Dolbear, of Tufts College demonstrated the exact system of wireless that Marconi demonstrated fourteen years later. This system was a long way short of the radio system that resulted from Tesla's ideas.

In 1893, before the prestigious Franklin Institute in Philadelphia Pa., Tesla gave a lecture that completely described the modern radio. He presented the idea for a ground connection, an antenna, an aerial-ground circuit containing inductance and capacity, an adjustment for tuning, sending and receiving sets tuned in resonance, and electronic tube detectors. These, together with the loudspeaker Tesla had invented while still in Europe make a complete working radio system. Two years later, Sir Oliver Lodge demonstrated a wireless system of transmission before the British Association for the Advancement of Science at Oxford. Two years after Lodge, Marconi presented his system, which was essentially the same as Lodge's system, and the system demonstrated fourteen years earlier by Professor Dolbear. All three were using short wave. After difficulties with short wave radio became apparent the system changed to the longer waves that Tesla had suggested previously. Then, as radio developed, two things occurred. One was a change to the tuning system of Tesla and the second was broadcasting, as Tesla had originally proposed. These completed the key developments. Not only was the system proposed by Tesla much

27

more advanced then the system of Marconi, but Marconi had used several inventions patented by Tesla to develop his system. Tesla never enforced his patents against Marconi, but Marconi tried to get his claims approved in court. It was not until after Tesla died that the Supreme Court upheld Tesla's priority in the invention of radio.

During the following years, Tesla led a colorful, productive life, but was constantly beset by money problems. He did not defend his ideas, and others made fortunes from ideas he was too busy to develop. He patented all manner of inventions, even several that are fundamental to computers. Characteristically, he rarely put his ideas to paper. That is why his most intriguing idea seems to be lost. Tesla indicated that a system of power from electrical energy in the Earth, could be tapped any where by simple portable devices. If anyone else proposed such an idea there would be no reason to take him seriously. But Tesla was the electrical genius beyond all others. At his death during World War 2, government agents seized his papers. (Tesla had done work with military applications, such as remote control robot boats and airplanes). Some say the system was described in his papers, and because vested power interests would be ruined, the system was not made public. Others say that Tesla put so little in writing that no one can unravel the mystery. Still others say that Tesla had lost touch with reality by the time of his death. Perhaps someday a new genius will develop this potentially world shaking idea. For now, we can straighten out the record on radio, the alternating current power system, remote control, and to some extent computers, by recognizing the contributions of this great genius.

What You Know...

When a prophet is proved wrong, his believers become disenchanted

...that is not so

Many of the world's great religions are based on prophecies that failed. Could that happen to modern rational people? What about scientific prophecies? Would modern rational people continue to follow failed prophets?

William Miller, a Baptist preacher proclaimed that the second coming of Christ would occur on October 22, 1844. When that day passed uneventfully, his followers split into those loyal to him and the disillusioned. Those loyal became affiliated with the Millerite church. One of the features of the Millerites was observing the Sabbath on Saturday, the seventh day, instead of Sunday. As the church grew and other congregations formed, the church adopted the name "Seventh Day Adventists". Today the church is a vigorous, growing, world wide group with headquarters at Battle Creek Michigan.

The faith in some pseudoscientific prophecies can also remain unshaken although the prophecies fail to occur. Doomsaying, in particular, seems to have a charm for humankind, no matter how often it fails. The sign proclaiming the end of the world is a trite joke if dressed in religious garb, but give it a scientific garb and even well educated and powerful people will succumb. Actually the prophets give it an anti-scientific garb, since the common theme is "limits to technology, or limits to growth".

Consider the stunning prophecies of population control advocates. In 1968, a best selling book[4] predicted the growth of human population would so outrun the growth of food production that world wide starvation would begin within nine years. That meant by the year 1977, if nine years is added to the publication date. The next year in Ramparts Magazine a spokesman predicted the death of the ocean by 1979. By that he seemed to mean that all life in the ocean would die. He had previously declared Lake Erie already dead. India, in particular, he singled out as an international basket case. In 1968 a spokesman said "I have yet to meet anyone familiar with the situation, who thinks India will be self sufficient in food by 1971, if ever." He said that unless population growth fell below replacement level there would be a massive die-off from starvation in 1990 and beyond.[5]

The reader may assume that these unrestrained exaggerations and shocking predictions were only done for effect, and that these advocates did not really mean them. That is not the impression that they gave at the time. Even today, spokesmen defend these predictions, claiming that by feeding the ever growing population we have only made the future still worse.

This modern doomsday's reasoning has an ancient pedigree. In 1798, Thomas Malthus proposed that the growing population would lead to starvation because the food supply could not grow as fast as population grows. The logic was inescapable, even though it was wrong. Followers of the original theory expected the world to run out of food a century ago. Instead, the problem of industrialized nations is food surplus.

Why is the Malthusian theory, and the modern restatement wrong? The theory derives from observation of animals. Animals reach an equilibrium with their environment when their population grows to the limit that the natural environment can sustain. Man, on the other hand, manipulates the environment to produce what he wants. Each person can produce more than he consumes. By technology and ingenuity, human beings create goods and services. Animals do not create or produce. Reasoning from analogy with animals is useless.

A classic example of the Malthusian kind of error occurred early in the twentieth century. The noted chemist Sir William Crookes predicted that the world's nitrate supply would be insufficient to maintain the fertility of the land. Fifteen years later Haber developed a method of nitrogen fixation from the atmosphere. This is an unlimited and inexhaustible supply.

Furthermore, humans can control their reproduction. If it is not to their advantage to have children, rational humans can limit the number of children born.

It is instructive to note that lower population areas like Ethiopia are the areas with food problems. The densely populated areas like Japan and Holland are well fed. India had starving masses when it had a population of 350,000,000 fewer people then it has today. Today it feeds itself. The only correlation with population density is opposite what the Malthusian theory claims.

The notion that people are a kind of pollution on the planet became the trendy idea for Hollywood celebrities and similar groups. They are embarrassed by riches that they may secretly believe they do not merit. A kind of cognitive dissonance develops. They fervently believe in mutually contradictory ideas. That is why a meeting of Hollywood environmental activists can make speeches about how to save the Earth by conservation, while their chauffeurs are idling the motors on the limos that are waiting in line to drive them to the luxury and extravagance of their local mansions

When the world did not starve, and the seas did not die, did these doomsayers fade into obscurity? Not any more than a religious zealot when the second coming does not happen. Many new books continue to sell. Recently a guest was making regular doomsday pronouncements on the NBC network "Today" show, as a special report on the environment. International meetings attended by world leaders meet to discuss the problem of world population growth. The prestigious Club of Rome and a group called

31

Zero Population Growth (ZPG) spread similar ideas. It is the people who pointed out the error in these doomsday's predictions that are faded into obscurity.

What You Know...

The guillotine was used to kill its inventor, Dr. Guillotine

...that is not so

The inventor of the guillotine was named Antoine Louis. He died of an infected carbuncle at age seventy-six.

What You Know...

Nazi Germany started the use of concentration camps

...that is not so

Britain used them during the Boer war.

What You Know...

The United States is a young government

...that is not so

Almost every country in the world has had a major change in government since the United States formed. Instead of being a young government, the United States is one of the oldest.

What You Know...

The Communists overthrew the Czar

Czar

...that is not so.

<u>1. War with Japan creates a strong movement against the Czar.</u>

At the beginning of the twentieth century, Russia, under Czar Nicholas, was expanding it's influence into Manchuria and towards Korea. This brought them into conflict with Japan. In February 1904 Japan launched an attack on Port Arthur in the Yellow Sea, similar to the attack launched 37 years later at Pearl Harbor. Both took place while diplomatic talks were proceeding, and both took place without warning.

The eighteen month war was a continuous disaster for Russia. Port Arthur, a fortress that like Singapore during WW2 was considered impregnable, surrendered while it still had adequate food and ammunition. In a desperate gamble, Russia launched an aged Baltic fleet at Japan, and saw it massacred off the coast of Tsushima Island.

The war went poorly, and as the morale of the army fell, the conditions at the home front worsened still more. During the Russo-Japanese war, Czar Nicholas faced many demands for reform of his autocratic, oppressive government. His troops fired on demonstrators outside the winter palace, and killed hundreds. Strikes and riots began throughout Russia. The Japanese met with most revolutionary leaders in Russia to support and finance a revolution[6]. In an attempt to appease the people, the Czar promised a representative assembly, or Duma. Following more problems, including; a mutiny by the crew of the warship Potemkin, a general strike, riots and turmoil throughout the empire, and the complete defeat in the war with Japan, the Czar regained control by using his troops against the revolutionists. He reiterated his promise to establish a Duma.

Not only had the Czar lost prestige in the world, damage to his armed forces, and collapse of his dreams of a new empire in the east, but the war had brought the Russian underground new vigor. The conditions for revolution were created. The Czar was in more danger from his own people than from the Japanese.

Before the first Duma met, the government limited the legislative powers of the Duma, and reserved autocratic powers for the Czar. The Duma was dissolved after only two months. A second Duma met in 1907 and was also dissolved. After revolutionary pressure began to mount the government applied severe repressive measures.

A more conservative movement dominated the third Duma. It enacted reform legislation.

2. World war brings famine to Russia

After the assassination of Archduke Ferdinand, Russia refused to allow Austria to invade Serbia. The first world war started. The fourth Duma was supportive of the Russian government in the war.

The Czar had huge forces to throw at the enemy, but after a short time, lack of supplies, lack of transport, and poor military leadership assured a military disaster.

Refugees flooded the cities from the front. Famine threatened. Discontent spread through the populace, and the soldiers. In the trenches, soldiers fought without food, shoes, and even without munitions.

3. Czar loses support of the nobility.

Many blamed military defeats on the monk Rasputin, who had achieved a dominant influence on the superstitious Czarina. Talk of the need to overthrow the Czar to save the monarchy became widespread at court. The hatred that surrounded the German born princess and the strange monk that dominated her had grown into an hysteria that extended even to the aristocracy. A group of avid monarchists felt that the assassination of Rasputin was needed to save the Czar. The conspiracy included; Prince Yusupov, scion of a rich and noble family, Grand Duke Pavlovich, a cousin of the Czar, right wing leaders of the Duma, a fashionable army doctor, and others who wished to save the Czar. They invited Rasputin to supper at the home of Prince Yusupov. There they fed him cakes poisoned with cyanide of potassium and wine, also laced with poison. Hours went by and Rasputin showed no sign of the poison. The superstitious plotters feared Rasputin's supernatural powers. They prayed before a crucifix, and then Prince Yusupov shot Rasputin in the heart. Rasputin fell back upon a bearskin rug. At first he seemed to be dead, but like a character in a horror movie, he rose and tore off an epaulette from the shoulder of Prince Yusupov. Rasputin scrambled through a locked door into the snow covered courtyard. Purishkevich chased Rasputin firing shots. Two times his bullets struck Rasputin, who fell again. The conspirators beat the body, but life still sparked in Rasputin. The conspirators dragged the body into the house, where they bound and gagged Rasputin. Then they drove him to the river and cast the bound body into the water. When the body was found several days later, reports circulated that Rasputin had freed himself before drowning. Water in his lungs indicated he was not yet dead when cast into the river. Hard as he was to murder, at last he was dead. Learning that Rasputin had been assassinated by a group of aristocrats, the Czar responded by favoring Rasputin's followers at court.

4. Provisional government forms.

Food shortages in Petrograd (successively called Leningrad and now St. Petersburg) caused mobs to take to the streets. This lead to violent encounters with the police, and a general strike. Cossack troops were sent to support the police, but did not take an active part. The police went into hiding.

Troops from the nearby garrison were sent in. At first they fired, killing many strikers. The strikers returned to the streets after the troops ceased firing. Many of the strikers tried to proselytize the troops. Some of the regiments joined the revolution.

No sooner had the Czar dissolved the Duma, then the deputies reassembled as "the provisional committee of the state Duma". By the next day, the entire garrison had gone over to the revolution.

A provisional government formed by the provisional committee of the state Duma took over the government. At the same time the socialists formed a representative body of deputies which was called a soviet. A self appointed group formed an executive committee of the soviet, and became its spokesman. At this time the Bolshiviks were a small minority in the soviet.

When the Czar attempted to go to Petrograd to consider proposals for a new government, a message from the Duma claimed the Duma was in power. The Czar's train was diverted, and the generals indicated they were willing to submit to the Duma. The Czar abdicated in favor of his brother, the Grand Duke Alexandrovich. The grand duke refused the crown, unless it was offered by a future constituent assembly. The provisional government took over the country.

Key figures in the provisional government included Prince Lvov, as Prime Minister Paval as Minister Of Foreign Affairs, and Alexander Kerensky as Minister of Justice. Although Alexander Kerensky had been a member of the executive committee of the soviet, none of these were Communist, and all expected to develop a republic eventually. The Petrograd soviet joined the provisional government in a statement that the provisional government was to rule in the place of the Romanovs until a constituent assembly could be elected by the people.

Thus it can be seen that the Czar was overthrown by a popular revolution and replaced by a non Communist government. The first Communist dictator, Lenin, at this time was not in Russia.

At first this provisional government was popular. The Petrograd soviet and the military both supported the new government. The government, however hesitated to take significant action, because it was only provisional. It also felt that a true election should be put off until the war was ended.

5. Lenin retuns to Russia from Germany..

As the misery of the populace continued from the war shortages, and the various political factions squabbled for power, the German high command fired a figurative cannon ball into Russia. They released Lenin, and sent him into the chaotic situation just as purposely as any other aggressive act of war. Churchill described the shipping of Lenin into Russia as follows. "In the middle of April 1917 the Germans took a sombre decision. Ludendorff refers to it with bated breath. Full allowance must be made for the desperate stakes to which the German leaders were already committed. They were in the mood which had opened unlimited submarine warfare with the certainty of bringing the United States into the war against them. Upon the western front they had from the beginning used the most terrible means of offense at their disposal. They had employed poison gas on the largest scale and had invented the flammenwerfer. Nevertheless it was with a sense of awe that they turned upon Russia the most grisly of all weapons. They transported Lenin in a sealed truck like a plague bacillus from Switzerland into Russia"

Lenin arrived more then a month after the Czar had been overthrown. Many factions were pulling at the government. The decision to continue the war was particularly unpopular.

When Lenin arrived, he found the Bolshivik party in the process of forming a united front with the Mensheviks and social revolutionaries. There was no plan to seize power. Lenin outlined a plan to use propaganda to gain wider support. He also opposed all supporters of the war. Within a month he had persuaded the majority to his side.

39

6. Provisional government continues war.

The government attempted to satisfy the allies with ambiguous declarations for the war. They only succeeded in provoking more dissatisfaction in the populace. Although it succeeded in putting down an attempt to start a Civil War led by counter revolutionary General Kornilov, the government had to reorganize. Kerensky became minister of war.

Alexander Kerensky ordered an offensive which ended in complete defeat. Discipline in the military broke down even further. Millions deserted.

Demonstrations against the war grew to a size that startled even the Bolshiviks. The Bolshiviks took the opportunity to join the demonstrators, and by promising to keep the demonstration peaceful gained control of the mobs.

The government reorganized again. Kerensky was made Prime Minister. He reacted to the demonstrations with force. Lenin went into hiding, and Lenin's second in command, Trotsky was arrested.

Now the government further weakened as anti Bolshivik forces plotted against the government because they feared a new political alignment was forming.

General Kornilov led his troops into Petrograd ostensibly to save the revolution, but some believe to establish a dictatorship. He was opposed by Alexander Kerensky, the garrison in Petrograd, and the various worker groups. Kerensky allowed the Bolshiviks to be armed as they supported his government against General Kornilov. Kornilov's army dissolved before it reached the capitol, but the Bolshiviks held on to their weapons.

7. Communists under Lenin overthrow the provisional government.

Alexander Kerensky reorganized the government again. He formed a five man directory with himself as the head. Russia was proclaimed a republic.. Under pressure from the soviets, Alexander Kerensky released two major Communist leaders, Trotsky and Kamenev.

Lenin and Trotsky organized an attack on the headquarters of the provisional government. Kerensky escaped and went into exile.

Thus, the Communists overthrew a government that could be characterized as democratic. The Communists did not overthrow the Czar.

Economics is the one subject in which teachers can use the same final exam every year. They do not have to change the questions...they change the answers.

What You Know...

The Great Depression was caused by the stock market crash of 1929

...that is not so

The cause or causes of the Great Depression have been debated by commentators for years. There are many ideas on this subject. Events since 1929 have clearly demonstrated that the debacle on Wall Street was not the cause.

In 1987 a stock market crash occurred that rivaled the crash of 1929. Fears of another great depression swept the nation. Instead, the economy held steady. Nothing like the catastrophe of 1929 occurred. What was different?

A better question might be, what was different about 1929. There have been severe downswings in the economy periodically ever since the nation was founded. These panics, as they were called, were short and self correcting. Never before had a panic spread so deeply as to cause 25% unemployment. Never had a panic spread across the globe to the rest of the modern nations. Never had it lasted so many years. Never had a panic caused such widespread despair.

Those of us too young to remember can only get a glimpse of depression conditions by looking at today's homeless. Today, most of these are alcoholics, mentally ill, or drug addicts. In the depth of the depression, huge numbers of normal, hard working, family oriented people lived under conditions that were even worse than today's homeless. A safety net to help these victims was practically nonexistent.

43

Hitler's rise to power was assisted by German despair during this world wide depression. It came only a few years after a catastrophic inflation had wiped out the life savings of most Germans. A reasonable case can be made that the depression was a major cause of World War 2.

Why was the Great Depression so much worse than any before or since?

My investigation uncovered the amazing answer. Interviews with knowledgeable economists and other students of the great depression demonstrate that the unique factor that had not been present at previous depressions was the Federal Reserve system.

At first, it seemed ironic that the Federal Reserve Bank should have been at fault. The Federal Reserve Bank had been created in 1913, for just the purpose (we were told) of controlling and moderating the swings from boom to bust. In the first test of the Federal Reserve Bank, it seems to have worsened the swings. It failed. The only question is, did the Federal Reserve Bank cause the depression on purpose, or by incompetence?

There are two schools of thought. Those who blame incompetence tell a story of jealousy and struggle for power between the New York and Washington branches of the Federal Reserve Bank. Benjamin Strong had been one of the prime movers to push Congress to create the Federal Reserve Bank. He was President of the regional bank in New York. Benjamin Strong dominated the Federal Reserve Bank until his death. Then jealous rivals in Washington reversed his policies. The new policies precipitated the depression. Then when the stock market crashed, they persisted in draining liquidity from the system just as it was most needed. The result was the Great Depression.

During the 1930's a Congressional committee demanded the impeachment of the Federal Reserve governors. They said the Federal Reserve Bank had caused the stock market crash by pulling about one third of the money supply out of the economy. The central bankers foreclosed on vast numbers of indebted Americans and small banks.

The above school of thought can point to the action of the Federal Reserve Bank following the 1987 crash. During the panic, Federal Reserve Bank chairman Alan Greenspan was on the phone to major banks telling them to make loans as needed, the Federal Reserve Bank would back you up. He stemmed the liquidity crunch and averted disaster. These actions stand in stark contrast to the actions of the Federal Reserve Bank in 1929.

A factor that I have never heard mentioned is the effect of prohibition in precipitating the crash. Farmers who had been selling grains to the breweries now had no market. These first victims of government policy failed in large numbers. Banks that dealt with farmers were among the first to fail. By combining the farm crises with the liquidity crunch, a strong case can be made that the depression was a result of governmental incompetence and misguided morality. The developing government moves against tobacco and guns could produce a similar result when combined with our current debt inflated dollar. (Tobacco employs 2 million people, generates $22 billion in taxes at all government levels, and pays out $30 billion in wages, according to Congressional testimony)

Especially ironic is the response of the public and it's representatives to the problem. Despite the fact that government actions had deepened the depression, more government was proposed to solve the problem. The various government moves failed to bring the economy back to health, but did calm the public. It was World War 2 that finally ended the depression.

I should point out that the Federal Reserve Bank is not the government. Strictly speaking it is a private bank. The Federal Reserve Bank is owned by its Board Of Governors, its twelve regional banks and its member commercial banks. No branch of the federal government owns any portion of the Federal Reserve Bank. Even though the President appoints the key members, the President is not privy to the secret meetings of the Federal Reserve Bank. Many actions of the Federal Reserve Bank are contrary to the President's own interest. Never the less the Federal Reserve Bank should be considered part of the government. It is a creation of Congress, and has powers that are constitutionally reserved to Congress. Because of its vast powers, it might best be considered as a second government.

The second school of thought has a more ominous tale to tell. They point out that the architects of the Federal Reserve Bank that met on Jekyl Island, Georgia in 1910 referred to themselves as conspirators. These representatives of J.P. Rockefeller and Rothschild met in secret, never even using last names.[7] These theorists point out that forming the Federal Reserve Bank was opposed by the Democratic party, but could never be passed by the Republicans. Only a democrat could ram it down the Democratic party's throat, with republican support. The Republican party was split when Theodore Roosevelt ran against his own hand picked successor, allowing Wilson to win. Wilson, against his own party pushed through the Federal Reserve. These conspiracy theorists believe the Republican election split was engineered primarily to create the Federal Reserve Bank.

The conspiracy theorists point out that the battle to control the money had been fought continually since the founding of the nation. The tries at a central bank had always ended in an inflation followed by a crash. Andrew Jackson had abolished the second central bank in the United States and paid off the national debt. The last central bank was abolished and the United States operated without a true central bank from that time to the founding of the Federal Reserve Bank in 1913. There were however, federal banks that had the power to inflate the currency. The various panics that periodically hit the nation can be traced to the inflation and deflation activities of these semi-central banks. To correct the problem, Congress established the Federal Reserve Bank.

Money created by the Federal Reserve Bank always is accompanied by debt. That is how the Federal Reserve Bank creates money. Because the Federal Reserve Bank creates money as federal debt, the national debt can never be eliminated. The national debt gives a cover for the actions of the Federal Reserve Bank. It can manipulate the money supply to inflate and deflate the money supply, always blaming the national debt for inflation and high interest rates, even though the only real cause is the maneuvering of the Federal Reserve Bank.

Conspiracy theorists quote a variety of sources to show that the ultimate goal of the conspiracy is domination of the political system of each country and the world economy by a system of central banks acting together.[8] By alternately inflating and deflating the nation's money, the conspiracists could gradually gain control of all real assets, after the economy goes into a 1929 like crash. Then a panic stricken populace would go along with government taking away all freedom

The reason the Great Depression was created by the central bank was to soften the nation for new non-constitutional government that would be amenable to a new world order. During the great depression, freedom loving Americans willingly gave up many of their freedoms to let the government fight the depression.

Be it incompetence or conspiracy, the actions of the Federal Reserve Bank are at the heart of the ups and downs of the economy. It was not a stock market crash that caused the Great Depression; it was actions of the Federal Reserve Bank.

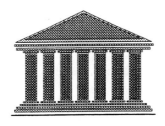

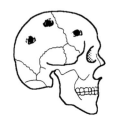

What You Know...

Brain surgery is a modern invention

...that is not so

The idea that ancient savage people could perform brain surgery boggles the mind. They had no anesthesia. They did not understand about germs. They probably had little conception of the function of the brain. Certainly if they had the temerity to open a skull of a living human being, only disaster could ensue. And yet...

At the College of Physicians and Surgeons in Philadelphia, Pennsylvania, there is a museum of medical artifacts. One wall has a display case of plaster casts of pre-Columbian skulls, each with one or more holes bored into it. A careful examination of these skulls shows that healing occurred after the hole was bored. Furthermore, some skulls were drilled open several times and healing occurred after each operation. In some way, these primitive savages successfully performed brain surgery.

The skulls were probably opened to let evil spirits out. It is inconceivable that anything was done to the brain itself. Yet successfully opening the skull with out killing the patient is amazing. Brain surgery has apparently been around a long time. This is not the first time researchers have been astonished by the achievements of ancient man.

What You Know...

Buffalo Bill's heroics were mostly the invention of a dime novel author

...that is not so.

It is very difficult to separate fact from fiction in the history of Buffalo Bill. He was named as the subject of several books that spread his fame, but some of these books were unreliable. Ned Buntline (Edward Judson) described Cody's heroics in two dime novel sensations, but the stories were really accounts of adventures lived by Wild Bill Hickock. Other authors made up adventures for Buffalo Bill to fill in gaps in his history. Buffalo Bill himself was quite willing to take credit for heroics performed by his friends, such as Wild Bill Hickock and Major Frank North. Peculiarly, these two did not resent this. They even encouraged the Buffalo Bill legend. Buffalo Bill was also a practitioner of the western game of telling tall tales around the camp fire. As happens when tales are repeated and embellished even the story teller cannot separate fact from fancy. Nevertheless, after stripping away the doubtful heroics, enough true heroics are left to make Buffalo Bill quite a guy.[9]

Buffalo Bill's real name was William Cody. His father, a fervent abolitionist was murdered by a pro slaver who stabbed him in the back. Cody took responsibility for the support of his mother and sisters at the age of eleven. He became a cattle herder in a wagon train, and took part in battles with Indians. Later, as a youth he rode in the Pony Express. This highly dangerous career has been the subject of many fact based films and stories, extolling the heroics of the Pony Express riders.

49

At the beginning of the Civil War he was a government scout and guide. In 1863 he enlisted in the 7th Kansas cavalry and fought in a few minor engagements.

Cody contracted with the Kansas Pacific Railroad to furnish buffalo meat to the workers on the line. This earned him his nickname.

He became chief scout of the United States army from 1868 to 1872. As a civilian he was awarded the Congressional Medal Of Honor, for his bravery and skill as a guide during a battle with an Indian camp. Later Congress rewrote the rules for the Congressional Medal Of Honor, restricting it to members of the armed forces. Because he won it as a civilian, his name was stricken from the role of medal winners, but it has since been returned to the role by act of Congress, along with four other civilians.

He was elected to the Nebraska Legislature in 1872.

He returned to scouting with the Fifth United States Cavalry in the Sioux war of 1876. Following the massacre of Custer, he led a small party that intercepted a large war party that was set to join the victorious Sioux forces. If the Indian forces had joined, the resulting army would have been formidable. In a man to man combat with Chief Yellow Hand, he slew the Indian chief and diverted the reinforcements.

During his scouting days Bill lived through numerous incidents that would make a man a hero in anyone's eyes.

He organized his "wild west show" in 1883, and became world famous as he took the show to Europe four years later.

In his later years he became an outspoken advocate of Indian rights, women's rights, and conservation.

With all of these legitimate achievements, why do most people believe Cody's heroics were mostly fiction? His name was used as the hero's name in two novels that were based on another man's exploits. Thus they were fiction as far as they pertain to Cody. This, combined with the usual hype of show business related to his wild west show cause the public to believe his whole reputation was mostly fiction.

Part Two

Things You Know About Science That Are Not So

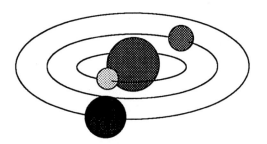

What You Know...

Water always boils at 212 degrees Fahrenheit

...that is not so

The boiling point changes with changes in pressure. Pressure changes with changes in altitude. At the top of Mount Everest, water boils at 167 degrees.

What You Know...

Acid rain is ruining our lakes and forests

...that is not so

As fish in mountain lakes began to disappear and forests grew yellow and died, a theory developed that acid rain was the cause. Acid rain is rain that has been contaminated by pollution from industrial by-products emitted into the air. Power plants and factories produce smoke that may contain sulfur and other chemicals that acidify the air.

Congress authorized an expensive research project to learn how serious the problem was. Even while the National Acid Precipitation Assessment Project (NAPAP) was gathering the facts, a move to regulate the problem was proposed. President Bush, determined to be the "environmental President", pushed the most sweeping regulatory law in history, the Clean Air Act of 1990. The equally environmentally sensitive Congress quickly passed this law.

The law could harm our industry in international competition and cost jobs and raise prices, but if it protected lakes and forests, that was a trade-off that a rich nation might make. However, even before the Clean Air Act passed the NAPAP preliminary reports cast doubt on the need for such expensive regulations. The report found acid rain a minor factor in the problem.

The scientists found that insects and plant diseases were the cause of problems in forests. Even more astonishing, the scientists found that the cause of fish disappearing from the lakes was the early environmental law of 1915 that forbid logging in the effected watersheds. It seems as though the soil around the lakes is the source of the acid. The lakes had not been good habitats for fish when the land was wild. During the slash and burn logging era, the fish thrived because alkaline ash neutralized the acid. Now the lakes are reverting to acidic, and fish no longer thrive. Acid rain can not be blamed for any significant part of the problem.

Neither Congress nor the President like to look foolish. They passed an expensive, harmful law that may be of little value. A vigilant media might expose this fiasco, except most of the media pushed for the law as hard as the politicians.

What You Know...

The earth is not the center of the universe

...that is not so.

Almost every educated person will assure you the Earth is a mere piece of dust floating around an ordinary star that is itself floating at an obscure edge of an ordinary galaxy. The sun is not special nor is the galaxy. Modern science has downgraded man's place at the center of the universe. Man is just a parasite on the fleck of dust that is the Earth. The idea that the Earth is at the center of the universe is ridiculous.

Yet the universe is described as infinite. There is a certain logic to an infinite universe. If a given point be called the end of the universe, then what lies beyond? Today, many scientists change the description of the size of the universe. It is frequently described as finite but unbounded.[1] For location of the Earth at the center, both concepts are equivalent.

If the concept of an infinite, or finite but unbounded universe is considered carefully, than the Earth must be at dead center. Consider any direction from the Earth. All will be the same. There will be an infinity to the edge of the universe in all directions. That puts the Earth at dead center. Of course the same can be said for any point in the universe. Every point in an infinite or unbounded universe is dead center. That is one of the peculiarities of infinity or unboundedness.[2]

Skeptics often say that astronomically speaking man is an insignificant microbe on an insignificant fleck of dust. But it can also be said that astronomically speaking man is the astronomer. From your position at dead center of this vast universe, who is right?

The position of the Earth at the center of the universe leads us to another startling concept. The concept is called the Anthropic Principle. The Anthropic Principle is science's answer to a series of discoveries, all of which, in their own way, focus on the unique position of humankind in the universe.

At first the discoveries seemed ordinary, but as they mounted up they became remarkable, and then unbelievable, until the Anthropic Principle returned these discoveries to inevitable and predictable.

Every time science considered a feature of the natural world, its importance to the existence of humanity became manifest. If the Earth orbited at a different distance from the sun, or the sun was hotter or cooler, or larger or smaller; if water unlike just about every other substance, didn't expand on freezing, or the Earth had as little water as the other planets, we would not exist. The odds against the first life forming by accident are so long that the entire history of the universe, even adjusted by a plethora of planets, is far too small to allow for chance, yet here we are. If the force of gravity were more or less then it is, the stars would not radiate for billions of years, nor would a planet orbit within the band of temperatures suitable for life. If the strong nuclear force was weaker, only hydrogen would exist, if it were stronger then carbon and oxygen would not exist.[3] If the ratio between the strong and weak forces were a little different, either hydrogen nuclei would fuse into helium or the reaction could not take place. In one case there would be no stars, in the other case, stars would have burnt up so quickly that life would not have had time to evolve.[4] The amount of carbon available for carbon based life (like us) to exist depends on the fortuitous energy level of helium-beryllium, which is just exactly right to speed along an otherwise improbable reaction. If the energy level was different there would not be sufficient carbon synthesized by "nature" for life, as we know it, to have developed.

The foregoing is just a taste of the unique properties that must be just so, or humankind would not be here.

When the number of special properties started to amass, religious thinkers argued that only a special creation could account for them. Scientists came back with the unanswerable, irrefutable Anthropic Principle. The Anthropic Principle declares that all these wonderful special properties are the way they are because we are here. The Anthropic Principle says that there could be any number of worlds. But humankind can only exist on a world with these special properties. Since we do exist, when we study properties of matter we must find those compatible with our existence. No matter how startling and unlikely a fact may be, it must be compatible with our existence.

One is reminded of the situation that existed among religious individuals when the "antediluvian" fossils started to appear. How could they account for dinosaurs and other creatures that seemed to have existed before creation? Here too, an undeniable, irrefutable answer was given. God, they said, is like the author of the world. When an author creates characters, he does not start at the first incident. He starts in the middle of the thing. Everybody is created with a history. The lead characters of a novel have a past that occurs before the novel starts. The hero of a novel is not a blank slate at the beginning. He has a mother who loved him, a father who beat him. All these shape the hero, but do not appear in the story. In the same way, the Earth had a history before creation. Dinosaurs were part of the history before the true creation. When God created Adam he gave him a navel, even though he was not born of woman.

Both the creation in the middle of history, and the Anthropic Principle explain anything, and explain everything, while at the same time, in another sense, they explain nothing. To a neutral observer, it is amusing that both science and religion have come to such common ground.

What You Know....

Mountains were raised many millions of years ago, today they are eroding away

...that is not so

There are some ancient mountain ranges that are eroding away, but many of the mountain ranges are rising at this time.[5] Ranges that are still rising include mountain ranges in the United States, such as the Rockies, the Cascades, and the Tetons.

The forces that cause mountains to rise are only beginning to be understood. As is common in science, a non-specialist gave the most important idea to a scoffing orthodoxy. He was laughed out of court until the weight of evidence and the death of all the old guard over time allowed his idea to triumph.

Alfred Wegener was a meteorologist, not a geologist. He noted that the outlines of the various continents fit together like a jigsaw puzzle. He thought perhaps the continents had drifted apart, after having once been joined together.

Much evidence to support Wegener was found. If the bulge of Brazil was fitted into the underbelly of Africa below Nigeria the fit was obvious. Fossils found on both continents were similar. Geologic formations ran across the divide. Even evidence of simultaneous glaciation was found.

However, Wegener could propose no mechanism to cause the drift of the continents. His work was lumped together with that of crackpots for generations.

At the same time, another anomaly appeared. The seas were supposed to be millions of years old. During those millions of years sediment fell to the bottom. Yet the amount of sediment was far too little. Deep sea exploration never found the vast layers of sediment that should have been at the bottom of the ocean.[6]

The solution was found during later deep sea exploration. The modern concept of plate tectonics is the continental drift theory of Wegener, updated. Geologists now believe there is a constant flow of lava up into the sea, spreading the ocean floor, and carrying the continents along. New sea floor is forming, old sea floor is disappearing into the deep-sea trenches. That is why the sediment is so shallow. The sea floor is young.

The plates carry the continents along. Where they butt up against one another, one rides up over the other. Earthquakes occur when one section slips along the other in a sudden release of pressure. Mountains are pushed up at these junctures. The Himalayas are forming as India collides with, and slips under Asia. Volcanoes form when the oceanic crust slips under a continent. The cascade range of the pacific northwest is forming that way.

Many of the great mountain ranges of the world are still forming, and still rising, some faster than others. For example, the highest mountain, 29,028 foot high Mount Everest, is rising slower than the ninth highest, 26,660 foot high Nanga Parbat. Geologist Nigel Harris of Britain's open University has been quoted[7] as projecting Nanga Parbit will grow higher than Everest over the next 150,000 years.

Most astonishing, is the hint that some of these mountain ranges have risen huge distances in recent times. For example, high in the Andes mountains, near Lake Titicaca, a great city has been found. The city is called "Tiahuanacu". It is at an elevation of 12,500 feet. It is surrounded by Agricultural terraces that are at elevations ranging up to 18,400 feet above sea level. At these altitudes it would be impossible to support the population that seems to have lived there when it was built. It is reasonable to believe that the mountains rose and lifted the city and agricultural terraces after the city was built. The city was probably a full mile lower when it was built.

During the lifetime of many people now living, a huge mountain sprang out of a Mexican cornfield and rose to majestic heights in a volcanic eruption. On February 20, 1943, a Mexican farmer in Paricutin, Mexico watched in amazement as a small fissure in his cornfield spouted steam and molten lava. Then violent explosions and ashes and light emitted from the fissure. Quickly it grew and formed a typical volcanic cone. The explosions increased, the lava flowed and the mountain grew. Spectacular fireworks increased as ash and glowing rocks flew into the air. By the time the volcano was 10 weeks old it had risen 1100 feet. Two hundred miles away in Mexico city the ash fell. The mountain lit up like a flaming candle as incandescent lava fragments formed the appearance of flame emitted from the rising cone, and shot up like a flaming geyser. By the end of the first year the mountain was 1500 feet high and still growing. A field of lava 10 square miles surrounded the mountain. Paricutin is about midway between Mexico city and the Pacific ocean, in Michoacan, Mexico.[8]

The extreme youth of mountains is not something just learned. As long ago as 1939 geologists proposed that the highest mountains in the world were so young that they had risen in historic times. The Swiss geologist, Arnold Heim, suggested that fossils and artifacts found on the Himalayas indicated that the last 3000 feet had risen during historic times.[9] Other geologists that reached similar conclusions before World War 2 were H. de Terra (Carnegie institute) and T. T. Patterson (Harvard University).[10]

Although the speed and extent of the uplifting can be debated, the fact that many mountains are still rising is now unquestioned.

What You Know...

Rubber tires insulate your car from lightning.

...that is not so

Lightning that jumps from a cloud to your car can easily jump from your car to the ground. The rubber tires do nothing. Your metal roofed car is, however, the safest place. The metal roof creates a ball of metal. Electricity will always stay on the outside of a metal ball.

What You Know...

Disposable diapers are more of a threat to the environment then cloth diapers

...that is not so.

Disposable diapers have been attacked as a threat to the environment because they do not biodegrade in solid waste landfills. It is certainly true that they do not biodegrade. However even newspapers do not biodegrade in landfills.[11] Forty year old newspapers were still readable when dug out of landfills. Landfills are designed to exclude air and other factors that would cause biodegradation.

What about cloth diapers? Are they safer for the environment. More important, are they safer for the baby?

Cloth diapers have to be washed. In todays working mother society, if cloth diapers were to be washed by commercial diaper services this would add to water pollution and increased energy use. The transportation to and from the laundry would add to air pollution. Use of cloth diapers results in more frequent rashes and infections from inadequate rinses. Cloth diapers are not an environmentally safer alternative.

The better question is, should everything be buried in solid waste landfills? Much solid waste, including disposable diapers can be better handled by composting. Modern municipal solid waste composting plants can convert about 60% of a community's garbage to nutrient rich soil enhancing sanitized compost in as little as one month.

Parents do not need to feel guilty about use of disposable diapers.

What You Know...

Invest in land, they are not making any more of it

...that is not so

The investment advice to invest in land has been good advice for most of the past half century, but the idea that "they are not making any more of it" is not so.

Great fortunes have been made by investing in real estate. There are many reasons why real estate has been a good investment. Some years real estate is attractive because of the financing available. A small down payment controls a valuable property. Any rise in value is multiplied as a profit on the small investment. If $10,000 down can buy a $100,000 property and the property rises in value 5% the investor has a $5,000 gain, on his $10,000 investment. This is a 50% gain on his original investment.

Another reason real estate may be a good investment is the pattern of growth that cities experience. People want to live or work in certain areas. The descendants of the farmers of early Manhattan island are now fabulously wealthy families.

Government restrictions on development can make the land that is available more valuable. If no one can build a home on the sea coast, the homes already there may become more valuable.

These are just some of the many reasons why real estate has been a good investment. Is it true that no land is now being made?

Geological processes are not too apparent in New York City. To see nature at work you must travel to less accessible parts of the world. Visitors to the great island of Hawaii can see the island growing as new land flows from the volcano. The entire chain of islands was originally created by the flow of lava.

TV and newspapers emphasized the destruction of homes as the glowing lava flowed over them. The flow to the sea where clouds of steam spurted over the glowing lava, made dramatic pictures shown on TV. The idea that new land was forming and the island was growing did not seem to register. This clash between the mighty volcano and the surging surf formed the entire chain of islands. Geology is not dead; history is not ended. The creation of the world is ongoing. They are making more land.

In November 1963, a sub sea volcano off the coast of Iceland blasted a column of smoke 3 miles high. Glowing lava, ash and exploding red hot rocks showered into the sea. Sulfurous rain cascaded down. Quickly a small island formed and grew. Within 3 years a square mile 560 foot high island was in the sea.

When enough surface cooled, life, in the form of bacteria, molds and algae invaded the sterile surface. Then birds and plants established themselves. In only a few years the island went through geologic changes that are supposed to require thousands of years. The amazed geologists saw gravel downs, calm lagoons, sand beaches and white cliffs appear. The island seemed to mature so quickly those Icelandic geologists now have a different opinion of the speed these changes occur, and the age of the world derived from geology investigation.

The island is named Surtsey, after the Icelandic Fire God Sutur.

Invest in real estate if you will, but not because They are not making any more of it.

What You Know...

Earthworms come out of the ground to avoid drowning in rainstorms

...that is not so

Earthworms love wet places. They come out to mate. If the ground is dry they stay deep in the damp Earth to avoid desiccation, and wait for the rain to allow them to come out safely.

What you know ...

The Earth goes around the sun

...that is not so.

The reader is probably so convinced of this scientific "fact" that a joke is expected. The entire history of the search for truth in this area of knowledge is fraught with misperceptions placed there by spin doctors. They told and retold the story of Copernicus, Galileo, Kepler, and Newton and buried the truth in myth. Now modern science in the form of Einstein's theory of relativity, has made moot the debate, but few realize this.

Before I offer the evidence that the Earth does not go around the sun, I will briefly summarize the history of the debate.

Although an ancient Greek called Aristarchis of Samos had proposed the sun as the center of the solar system, at the time of Copernicus, most people believed that the sun went around the Earth. The theory known as the Ptolemic theory, placed the Earth at the center of the solar system. This theory had difficulty conforming to the actual positions of the planets as observed by astronomers. It had to resort to epicycles, unnatural backward circles of motion by the planets to account for the observed positions. That is because planets appear to go forward part of the year, but reverse their passage and appear to go backward when the Earth passes them in their orbits. However, with these adjustments it worked quite well. It predicted where the sun, moon and planets would be, and even predicted eclipses and transits.

67

Copernicus promised in his book that his heliocentric theory would be simpler and would conform to observations even better than the Ptolemaic or geocentric theory.

The spin doctors would have you believe that Copernicus succeeded but that church fathers, because of biblical references, refused to accept the obvious.

The first problem with this is that Copernicus did not succeed in simplifying the motions. He had the planets moving in perfect circles. He had the planets move at uniform speeds during their orbits. He placed the sun at the center of the orbits. All of these do not conform to reality, and caused him to add more epicycles (circles on circles) to make the theory work. When it was published it was more complex than the geocentric theory.

The second problem was that if the Earth took these giant swings around the sun there should be some observed seasonal parallax. Parallax is the shift you observe between nearby objects and distant objects as you pass them. A nearby tree that appears to be on the left side of a far off hill shifts to the center and then the right side as an observer passes by. In the same way nearby stars should appear to shift position against the background of more distant stars as the Earth moved. No one could detect the slightest parallax, even though the Earth was moving an incredible distance if the theory was true.

Thirdly no one could detect centrifugal force that should be caused by the motion. This is the force that holds water in a bucket as you swing a bucket around on a rope. It is the force that keeps you pinned to the side as you spin on the amusement park ride. If the Earth was spinning then it should create centrifugal force. No one at that time understood gravity. (We still do not, but at least we have an idea about it)

These were only some of the scientific objections to Copernicus, that caused the church fathers to decline to overturn the teachings of Aristotle.

Aristotle? Yes, the geocentric theory was not biblical in origin. It was from pagan Greece. Although some scholars tried to give a biblical basis to one theory or the other, it was Aristotle and Ptolemy that gave the world the geocentric theory.

The church fathers were not stupidly adhering to an unscientific theory because the Bible said it so, they were rejecting an unscientific theory because reputable science said it was not so.

Kepler revamped the heliocentric theory of Copernicus. He changed the orbits to ellipses and varied the speed of the planets to sweep out equal areas as the planets move closer and farther from the sun. He moved the sun out of dead center to one focus of an ellipse. This simplified theory worked.

As the story was told and retold, the reasonable objections of the church became doctrinal religiosity. The church became a whipping boy, and the purported objection to rational science became a cause to attack religious faith. This was the spin put on the story as it became a myth.

Than came Einstein.

Some of the paradoxes that follow from relativity are favorites for writers about relativity. They love to blow our minds with the twin paradox. That's the one in which twins age at different rates because one travels at great speed, while the other stays at home.[12] Because time changes its rate as speed approaches the limit of the speed of light, the one twin ages while the other is still young. The change in rate has actually been detected by clocks sent into orbit, although the effect is quite small at speeds human beings have been able to achieve.

What does this have to do with the motions of the Earth and the sun?

The theory of relativity puts a completely new light on the subject. The concept of relativity includes a concept that all motion is relative to the observer. There is no fixed point against which all motion can be measured. It was in fact the search for a fixed point against which the motion of objects in space could be measured that led to Einstein's famous theory.

In one of the most astonishing experiments ever conducted, two experimenters, Michelson and Morley, found that the speed of light, as it passed the Earth measured almost exactly the same rate regardless of which direction it came from. If the Earth was moving through space the speed should be slower if coming behind the Earth, and faster if coming from the direction into which the Earth moved. The results of this experiment make no sense. Assume three trains traveling at 100 miles per hour, two going side by side in the same direction. The third train is coming toward the other two. The train going in the same direction would never pass the first train. It would just stay side by side as both trains are traveling at the same speed and going in the same direction. But the train coming toward them from the other direction would whiz right by at 200 miles per hour relative speed. In the same way, the speed of light should have measured differently if coming from the same direction as the Earth moved, then if coming from the opposite direction. Michaelson-Morley found the speed of light measured the same regardless of which direction the light came from.

When the astonishing results of Michaelson-Morley were published, there was no reasonable explanation, except that the Earth did not move. This could not be accepted. Einstein saved the day by taking the speed of light as absolute, and contrary to all common sense, making all motion relative. More exactly, Einstein said there is no way to distinguish between relative and absolute motion.[13]

The question of whether the Earth goes around the sun, or the sun goes around the Earth becomes moot. Either can be true, depending on the observer. We can continue to use the heliocentric theory because it is simpler to work with, but we can no longer say in some absolute sense that it is true.

Even when scientists predict eclipses, transits and other astronomical phenomena with astonishing precision, and even when

NASA fires rockets to the moon, mars and beyond, these do not prove that Ptolemy was wrong. The Ptolmiac, Earth centered theory could do these things also.

The reader may be further astounded to learn that this interpretation of the theory of relativity is not new. It was understood by scientists ever since relativity became established. In his authoritative 1922 book "Einstein's Theory of Relativity" Nobel prize winner Max Born said "thus from Einstein's point of view Ptolemy and Copernicus are equally right. What point of view is chosen is a matter of expediency." [14]

The concept of relative motion is a difficult concept, because we live on the Earth, and can measure any motion against a seemingly fixed Earth. Many people have sat on a train and watched the station seem to move away. The rider than forced a realization upon himself that the train was moving and not the station. The certainty that the train was moving and not the station came from the fixed Earth on which sits the station. If the station were floating in space the certainty that the station was not moving would cease. When objects are floating in space, the only way to determine motion is to compare the motion of each object to some other object. If all objects are floating, than motion might be measured against space itself. But there is no way to fix a point in space. With no fixed point, all motion becomes relative.

Now it should be understood, that any systematic description of the relative motion of Earth and sun in which Kepler's description of the motions was not used, would probably be so complex as to be useless. Then again, it might be possible to simplify and organize the motions with Keplerian precision, and have the Earth at the center. In any case, there is no fixed point against which motion can be measured. Since all motion is relative, the conclusion is that the Earth does not circle the sun, nor does the sun circle the Earth. Instead, we can only say, both have motions that can be described, by Kepler's laws. We assume the sun to be central only for simplicity.

The myth, however is still too useful to abandon. That is why the knowledge that the latest information has eliminated the question, and why the true story of the original argument remains buried.

In summary, under the theory of relativity, the question of does the Earth go around the sun, or does the sun go around the Earth is meaningless.

It will take generations until human minds can grow up with this concept. It took many generations for human minds to accept other concepts that also radically changed the relationships of man and nature. Consider that Newton published his Principia in 1687, yet more than 200 years later scientists were still rejecting the natural consequences of gravity. For example, if all objects pull on each other, why hadn't the stars all collapsed together? The universe had to be collapsing, unless it were expanding. The one thing it could not be was static.[15] Also, if it was expanding or collapsing it had to have a beginning. It could not have been eternal, although it could be oscillating. Yet these exact points were rejected by our most subtle minds right up to modern times. Even today, many consequences of what we know are kept hidden by our own preconceptions.

Nevertheless, there will come a generation raised with relativity as its natural view of nature. That generation will probably be as alien to us as the generation that debated in all seriousness, how many angels could stand on the head of a pin. That generation will intuitively understand relative motion, as we cannot.

Classical
Jazz
Rock and roll
Rap

Proof that evolution can be reversed

What You Know...

The survival of the fittest

...that is not so.

One of the great mysteries of the ages is adaptation. Just a quick look at the natural world impresses an observer of the almost miraculous adaptations that enable plants and animals to survive. Every living thing seems uniquely adapted to its life style and conditions.

Adaptations include protective coloration. Arctic animals are often white like the polar bear, so that they cannot be noticed against the snow. In other backgrounds stripes and spots hide the animals. Some insects are so well camouflaged they appear to be sticks or bird droppings. Others mimic dangerous, smelly or foul tasting creatures, even though they themselves are not dangerous, smelly, or foul tasting.

A duck's webbed feet are adapted to paddle in water. An eagle's talons are adapted to seize prey. A horse's hoofs are ideal for galloping over the plains, but a tiger's paw is shaped to aid the tiger kill its prey.

Carnivores can be identified by the teeth, designed to tear flesh. Herbivores can be identified by the teeth, designed to grind vegetation.

The night flying bat uses a sonar like adaptation to find its prey in the dark. Hawks on the other hand have eyes that can spot a mouse in the grass from high above. Animals that live where the range of vision is short, such as bears, have a keen sense of smell.

The internal chemistry of each creature is also adaptive. The photosynthesis of plants, the circulating blood of mammals, communication system of the nervous system, the workings of the digestive system, etc. are all adaptations. Recent work has given a picture of a fantastic and exquisite chemistry in higher animals. Only slight modifications in human chemistry are responsible for all manner of illness, malformation, and death.

Let us look at the adaptations needed by just one creature. Let us consider the woodpecker. As all birds, the woodpecker has light weight feathers for warmth, instead of the too heavy scales that it's purported evolutionary ancestors the reptiles have. It has hollow bones for strength with less weight. Unlike other birds it has a beak designed as a wood boring tool. (Imagine a woodpecker with a spoonbill. It would have starved to death at first creation). There are shock absorbers between the beak and the extra heavy skull. The tongue is long and slender, covered with barbs and a sticky substance. These adaptations enable it to reach into holes in trees and fish out insects. It has claws divided two forward and two backward, so the woodpecker can grip the bark of the tree while it pounds away. The tail feathers are unusually strong and steady the bird as it bangs into the tree. During molting the tail feathers do not fall out until enough feathers have been replaced to support the bird. The hearing is so acute that woodpeckers can locate insects under the bark by hearing. When it shares a need with other birds it shares the adaptation. When it has unique needs it has unique adaptations. All of its organs and behavioral adaptations are fully developed. None are half formed and developing.

The foregoing is just a slight smattering of adaptations. Every creature is a magnificent bundle of thousands of adaptations to enable it to cope. It will always have just the right equipment needed to cope. It would have to have just the right equipment, or it would have failed and become extinct long ago.

During the years before Charles Darwin published "The origin of species" there was a debate about how the different plants and animals came to be so well adapted to their life style and environment. The religious answer was simply "God made each creature to fit its place in the scheme of things." Those who preferred not to believe in God or sought a natural explanation, were hard put to find a solution. Most solutions proposed included an element of the supernatural, although one solution advanced was "inheritance of acquired characteristics". This held that events that occurred during the life of a creature could cause a change that was passed on to offspring. The giraffe stretched his neck to get at the higher vegetation. The giraffes' offspring would be born with longer necks.

Both experience and experiment have failed to confirm inheritance of acquired characteristics. For example, Jews have removed the foreskin from the penis of all their male children for 5000 or more years. The boys are born with the foreskin to this very day. Absence of foreskin would seem to be an acquired characteristic that should be inherited if the theory was true.

Darwin, and another naturalist, Wallace, both came up with a logical solution at the same time. They proposed that no offspring is exactly like its parents. Each exhibits a slight variation. It may be smaller or larger, darker or lighter. It may have a beak more curved or less curved. It may have more hair or less. These slight changes were random. There was no logic or purpose to them. However, nature would impose a purpose, because some variations would be better suited to the battle for survival. For example the moth that was harder to see because its color was close to the background color would survive longer than the moth with color that stood out against the background. The moth with the color closer to the background color would be more likely to procreate. The succeeding generations would have more of its progeny. Little by little the average moth would become colored to match the background. In this way, Darwin and Wallace proposed to explain adaptation.

The logic swept science off its feet. Here was a rational script to explain even the most dazzling adaptations. All that was needed was a lot of time, and random variations selected naturally by survival, would gradually change creatures from one species to another.

The expression "Survival of the fittest," coined by Spencer, was accepted by Darwin, and became a common shorthand for the process. This expression describes a process in which creatures deemed more fit survived to procreate more often then brother creatures deemed less fit.

When asked how to determine which was more fit, the measure was which survived. In other words the more fit survived because they were the survivors. There was no objective standard of fitness. Furthermore, when scientists looked at extinct animals, they sometimes seemed more fit then present day animals that had not become extinct. There was no rational basis to predict which would survive, and which would perish.

This became particularly noticeable when an animal like the horse was considered. The horse had become extinct in North America, but survived in other continents. If it was less fit, why did it succeed so well when Europeans reintroduced the horse in North America?

The wasp presented a classic problem for the proponents of the theory of the survival fittest. One species of wasp has a complex and amazing strategy for reproduction. It builds a nest. The wasp then goes out and stings caterpillars using just the right amount of venom to paralyze but not kill the caterpillar. The wasp stores the caterpillars in the nest. It lays eggs in such a manner that its newborn wasps are away from the caterpillar, and could not be hurt by the caterpillars writhing motions. The wasps hatch out and have fresh meat to eat while developing. If the caterpillar died while the wasp was incubating, the newborn wasp would not survive because the caterpillar would have rotted before the wasp could eat it. If the wasp placed the egg too near the caterpillar it would be crushed before the wasp attained sufficient size. To protect the egg the wasp hangs it from the top of the nest, so the baby wasp can eat a few bites without getting hurt itself. In an especially macabre touch the wasp baby eats only the portions of the caterpillar that will not kill the caterpillar. It saves the vital organs for last, so the meat stays fresh.

Among the problems to consider are; when the wasp was first developing this behavior, what happened until it got it right? Obviously for the first few million years the wasp injected too much venom and the caterpillars all died. The baby wasps hatched and the food was spoiled. These wasps all died as babies. Other wasps injected too little venom. The caterpillars escaped. The young of these wasps also died in the larva stage, because they had no food. Later generations laid the eggs too close and these all died as babies, crushed by the writhing caterpillars. What! Later generations? Yes, this is just one example of something that had to be right the first time.

The world is rife with examples of organs and behavior that had to be right the first time. There is a worm that swallows a stinging polyp without discharging the stinging cells. The polyps are moved through the digestive tract and positioned on the worm as defensive organs. Imagine this behavior developing tiny step by tiny step, each step an improvement, each step making the worm more fit.

The intricate behavior of parasite with host is also a problem for selection by survival of the fittest. The dog heart worm ultimately kills the dog. To survive, its larva must be carried by mosquito to another dog. To further complicate the picture, all three creatures evolved millions of years apart. Some parasite and host relationships involve different hosts for different stages of parasite development.

Any organ that developed as a new structure represents a problem. If a creature (such as a fish), without legs evolves legs, then each tiny increase in leg like appendage must be selected for survival value. What use is a fin that is almost a leg? It will not swim well, nor will it run well. Instead of helping it would hinder.

A turtle shell that is too soft to protect will only weigh down a more vulnerable turtle. By the time natural selection developed a hard shell, the turtle would be extinct. Moving the shoulder blades from outside its rib cage to inside its rib cage must have slowed down the turtle during all the intermediate positioning, as well.

Actually, many organs that are touted as necessary for survival appear in some creatures but are absent in others that also survive quite well in similar circumstances. Feathers are supposed to have evolved for flight, but bats do not have feathers, and fly quite well. Furthermore some birds with feathers cannot fly. The long neck of the giraffe cannot be essential for survival because young giraffes- survive while they are too small to reach the tops of trees. The females never achieve the height deemed essential for the males to survive. Both horned and hornless varieties of sheep survive today.

Earlier I wrote of the adaptations of the woodpecker. As if to go out of its way to prove that the entire concept of evolution by survival of the fittest is superfluous, a woodpecker with all the adaptations that seem so essential for woodpecker life style, survives with a completely different life style. Darwin was quite aware of this woodpecker. The following is his comment on woodpeckers.

"Can a more striking instance of adaptation be given than that of a woodpecker for climbing trees and seizing insects in chinks in the bark? Yet in North America there are woodpeckers that feed largely on fruit, and others with elongated wings that chase insects on the wing. On the plains of La Plata, where hardly a tree grows, there is a woodpecker...which has two toes before and two behind, a long pointed tongue, pointed tail feathers, sufficiently stiff to support the bird on a post, but not so stiff as in typical woodpeckers, and a straight strong beak...hence this (bird) in all essential parts of its structure is a woodpecker. Even in such trifling characters as the coloring, the harsh tone of voice, and undulatory flight, its close blood-relationship to our common woodpecker is plainly declared;

yet...in certain large districts it does not climb trees, and it makes its nest in holes in banks! In certain other districts, however...this same woodpecker...frequents trees, and bores holes in the trunk for its nest."

It should be apparent from the foregoing that millions of years of shaping by natural selection has produced a bird that can live quite well with all the wrong adaptations that were purported to be necessary for survival.

Wolves hunt in packs. The fastest wolf and the slowest wolf share the catch. The catch is usually an old or infirm member of the quarry. How can survival of the fittest select the fastest wolf, or the slowest prey?

Ants and bees are all sterile except for a queen. Any selection of traits effecting the workers cannot be inherited because the workers do not mate. Selection would have to choose the hive as a unit and not any individual ant or bee. Since ants practice farming, animal husbandry, war and slavery, while bees communicate by their dance, air condition their hive and build sophisticated honeycombs, the stress on selection becomes overwhelming. Remember selection cannot create, it can only preserve what blind chance has presented to it.

When plant and animal breeders practice artificial selection, some other problems with natural selection become apparent. Breeders find that constant attention is required or the plants and animals will revert to type in a few generations. Without an unnatural selection the process will not continue. Furthermore, breeders have never succeeded in breeding new species or new organs. Natural selection actually seems to work to maintain stasis, not develop new species.

Darwin explained the development of secondary sexual characteristics, such as male ornamentation as resulting from females choosing attractive traits from among various suitors. Some male fish exhibit colorful changes during mating season, but they fertilize the eggs without the female being present, or even aware fertilization is occurring. When can sexual selection occur?

Extinction, instead of comforting believers of survival of the fittest, presents a contradictory picture, that can only discomfort them. Over 90% of all species that have ever lived have become extinct. Although there are some extinctions occurring at any time, most became extinct during brief catastrophic events that eliminated the most fit and least fit at random. If there can be a concept of most fit, the survival because of fitness was not assured.

When the dinosaurs became extinct, they were not a senile moribund group with no more evolutionary options. Robert Bakker of Johns Hopkins University says they were vigorous and still diversifying into new orders. They were producing a variety of big-brained carnivores with the highest intelligence yet present on land. At the same time mammals were an ancient group that had been comparatively unsuccessful for most of the millions of years while the dinosaurs reigned supreme. The mammals had not demonstrated any greater fitness for 150 million years. Only when a catastrophe wiped out the dinosaurs and extinguished life on land and sea in prodigious numbers, did the mammals proliferate.[16] There is nothing to hint that mammals were fitter than dinosaurs, only that they were luckier. Here is how David Jablonski, of the University of Chicago put it. "Mass extinctions change the rules of evolution. When one strikes, it is not necessarily the most fit that survive; often it is the most fortunate. When their environment is disrupted, groups that had been healthy can suddenly find themselves at a disadvantage. Other species that had been barely hanging on squeak through and inherit the Earth. The best example is the mammals. Dinosaurs and mammals originated within 10 million years of each other, about 220 million years ago, but for 140 million years dinosaurs ruled, while mammals stayed small and scrambled around hiding in the underbrush. Mammals all basically looked alike-squirrely or shrewish and no larger than a badger- until the dinosaurs disappeared. Then they took off. Within 10 million years there were animals of all shapes and life styles; whales, and bats;

carnivores and grazers. Mammals just couldn't do anything inter-esting until the dinosaurs were out of the way."[17]

If extinction represents a problem for survival of the fit-test, so too does the persistence of living fossils. This seems like the opposite of extinction; non extinction. However, it is even harder to fit into the concept of survival of the fittest. As we saw above, extinction has no correspondence with fitness. Living fossils, how-ever, deny the very foundation of natural variation. If creatures can persist for millions of years without change, what can cause the change that caused the evolution of so many other creatures?

Imagine the surprise if a dinosaur walked down the streets of New York. When a Coelacanth (a species of fish supposed to be extinct for 70 million years), was found alive in the catch of fisher-men, the surprise was equivalent. "Here is one of the great myster-ies of evolution," said Jacques Millot, director of Madagascar in-stitute of scientific research.[18]

Creatures that have persisted unchanged for millions of years can be called living fossils. Many insects fall into this cat-egory. The cockroach has been dated to 350,000,000 years ago, unchanged. Fossils of the black ant have been found in remains dated 70,000,000 years ago.[19] Other types of creature that are liv-ing fossils include certain mollusks (once thought extinct 280,000,000 years ago), a giant reptile called the tuatara, scorpi-ons, and many plants such as cycads, ginkgo trees and ferns. Why did random variation and natural selection fail to occur in these and dozens of other living fossils?

The spider is supposed to have evolved its spinneret and web to catch flying insects. A fossil spider complete with spinneret has been found in strata that is dated millions of years before the evolution of flying insects. Why had the spinneret evolved, when there were no flying insects to snag?

After science lived with the idea of survival of the fittest for some years, the inadequacy of the concept became clear. Thou-sands of organs and behaviors were considered that could not have developed in this way. Darwin himself had recognized some of these. The eye in particular is so very complicated, and each part so interdependent that a development by slight incremental change, each change preserved because it is more beneficial, becomes unbelievable. No example of a developing but not yet fully developed organ has ever been convincingly shown. All organs seem to be fully developed when we encounter them.

Other problems arose when the fossil record became more complete. If each change was slight, and the changes took place over long periods of time, then the fossil record should be mostly intermediate forms. The theory holds that birds developed from the reptiles. Transitional forms between birds and reptiles should be more common then either birds or reptiles. The same should hold true for any of the macro changes. Instead the transitional forms are rare. Instead of slow changes the fossil record seems to show large changes occurring in a geological wink of an eye.

New explanations for evolution have been proposed. These do not have the beauty of Darwinian evolution, and are less comprehensible to the layperson. These new evolutionary theories allow for jumps in the fossil record. They conform more closely to the actual fossil history, but lack one major element. The apparent purposefulness of evolution is poorly accounted for. The adaptations that so enthralled our ancestors, are poorly explained. Jumps in organ structure occur, but there is no time for molding by natural selection. The new organ springs out ready to use.

The most widely discussed of these new theories is "punctuated equilibrium" proposed by Niles Eldridge and Stephen Gould. This theory places most evolutionary change in discontinuous rapid speciation. During long periods very little change occurs. Although both the author's of the new theory and the evolutionists in general seem to prefer to hide it, the theory of punctuated equilibrium is directly contrary to Darwin's theory. Darwin said such jumps are not allowed in his theory. Darwin once said, "If it could be demonstrated that any complex organ existed, which could not possibly have been formed by numerous, successive, slight modifications, my theory would absolutely break down."[20]

Evolutionists use the expressions "natural selection" and "survival of the fittest" like mantras and to prove their orthodoxy. It is a professional secret that the expression "survival of the fittest" is meaningless. Most evolutionists today would change the word "fittest" to "prolific". Evolution seems to have taken place, but how it happened is less clear then it seemed a few generations ago.

What You Know...

Trees live hundreds of years

...that is not so

Because the giant redwood tree lives for centuries, and the cypress lives even longer, trees have developed a reputation for living hundreds of years. Although some trees have long life spans, many trees do not. The life span of most of the fruit trees, for example, is only twenty to thirty years. Most common trees have a life span that is less than the life span of a human being.

Part Three

Things You Know About Health That Are Not So

Things You Know

Tee Shirt Wisdom

> Eat right
> Exercise
> Die anyway

What You Know....

Lose weight and live longer

.... that is not so

"You can't be too rich or too thin," is a famous aphorism. Perhaps you cannot be too rich but it is possible to be too thin. Two illnesses that cause a person to be too thin are anorexia nervosa and bulimia. Anorexics have a self image that they are too fat. They follow extreme low calorie diets. Bulimics eat or even binge on food, but cause themselves to throw up so they will not get fat. Victims of these diseases can look like emaciated concentration camp inmates. They starve themselves. Mortality rates are 15%.

Anorexia nervosa and bulimia are extreme cases. What about people who are just a bit underweight? What about people who are at or near ideal weight? Surely these people live longer than people who are overweight.

The causes of underweight and overweight may themselves effect mortality rates. For example, cigarette smokers claim that they gain weight when they stop smoking. Sub-clinical diseases can cause underweight. Various studies have attempted to correct for these causes of early mortality. These corrections tend to reduce the statistical mortality of underweight people.

Distribution of body fat also plays a part. Researchers associate fat on the upper body with increased mortality. Fat below the waist does not seem to be associated with increased mortality. In these cases the seemingly more athletic barrel chested build seems to be associated with higher mortality. The pear shaped build seems associated with lower mortality.

In 1983 Metropolitan Life Insurance Co. published new height and weight tables that raised ideal weight substantially above previously accepted tables. In 1990, based on actual mortality records, the Federal Government raised the desirable weights. There was an outcry from the "food police". They demanded the old tables be used. They said these higher weights would encourage people to indulge themselves by overeating.

What is your picture of a fat person? Lazy, self indulgent, subject to diabetes and heart disease? Obese people must surely die earlier than thin people.

This is not so. Population studies over and over again show that people 10-20% overweight live longer than people 10-20% underweight. These people even live longer than people at the previously accepted ideal weight.

A 32 year study of Dutch men showed the leanest men had the highest mortality.[1] A Finish study found the lowest mortality at a body mass index usually considered obese. A Kaiser Foundation study found no increased mortality association with weight.

Even worse news for the food police and weight loss was the result of a study of dieters published in American Journal of Epidemiology, September 15, 1992. *Subjects who lost over 15% of their weight increased the risk of mortality by two times over those with little or no weight loss.*[2]

Other studies have found hypertensive underweights at higher risk than hypertensive overweights.

There is a genetic component to weight and build. Identical twins raised apart have similar build and weight. Dieters tend to regain the lost weight quickly. The so called yo-yo dieters actually increase the risk of death by stressing the body with frequent weight loss.[3] Studies of caloric intake show little correlation to weight. In short, few people will gain in health by strict dieting.[4]

The conclusion is that underweight is a greater risk than overweight, and dieting is also a risk. The obese person should follow good health practices, but should also learn to accept his or her natural weight.

What You Know...

The dangerous thing about eating fruit and vegetables is pesticide.

...that is not so.

Ever since Rachel Carson published "Silent Spring" the danger of pesticides has become a subject for popular discussion. Well meaning but uninformed nonprofessionals protest any chemical sprayed on growing flora. A movie star tearfully protesting the chemical spray Alar was instrumental in getting it banned, even though it has never been found harmful in any government study. Alar is not a pesticide. It was sprayed on apples to improve appearance and quality. When it became a subject for debate, apple growers decided the only way to assure a doubtful public that apples were safe was to ban the use of Alar. The ban was not because any study had shown any danger from Alar.

DDT is another controversial chemical that was banned. After all manner of dangers to human beings were proven false, the ban was instituted because DDT was implicated in thinning the shells of certain birds of prey. The consequence of the debate over DDT is not widely known. The activists who worked so hard to ban DDT might not like to know how the ban affected human beings.

As one example, Ceylon had a history of two to three million cases of malaria at one time. By spraying with DDT Ceylon reduced the cases of malaria to almost zero. Then, influenced by "Silent Spring" and the United States' attacks on DDT, Ceylon stopped spraying with DDT. The mosquitoes came back, and malaria came back with a vengeance. Millions of cases of malaria could be traced to the ban on DDT. Naturally Ceylon resumed spraying.[5]

91

Most charges against chemicals used on our food imply that the chemical causes cancer. Cancer is not only an especially dread disease, it may take years to develop. The cause is usually unknown. It is easy to blame chemicals sprayed on our food for this disease and panic the uninformed consumer. The national cancer Institute and the Food and Drug Administration have looked into these charges. The statistics derived from their studies are enlightening.

Based on these authoritative sources, an article in *American Health Magazine*[6] published the following statistics: the risk of cancer from pesticides on food, 11 in 100,000. The risk from natural carcinogens (aflotoxins, etc.) occurring in food is 110 in 1,000. (That is 11,000 in 100,000, or one thousand times as high as the risk from man made chemicals sprayed on the food.)

If you did not know that natural carcinogens occur in food, do not blame yourself. There has been a conscious effort to deny this by the environmental alarmists. During the controversy, CBS "60 Minutes" did a report on Alar. One of the scientists that had been interviewed pointed out to the producer, the amount of natural carcinogens in food. The program not only downplayed this fact, the program attempted to discredit highly respected scientists who tried to put the risk into perspective.

The American Council on Science and Health annual sample menus include the harmful chemicals that naturally occur in our food. Chemicals that are toxic (deadly), carcinogenic (cancer causing) and mutagenic (causing birth defects) are in just about everything we eat or drink. The council lists Amylase Inhibitors, Arsenic, Chaconine Isoflavinese, Nitrate, Oxalic Acid and Solanine as harmful chemicals in the common baked potato. Broccoli contains Allyl Isothiocanate, Glucosinolates, Goitrin and Nitrate. The council produces lists of harmful chemicals in every food in a typical menu.

The fact that there are natural causes for cancer should not come as a surprise. Cancer did not start with the industrial revolution. Mummies from Egypt have tumors. Reports and descriptions of cancer are found throughout history.

Some naturally occurring carcinogens are the plants' reaction to insect attack. The pesticide that is so feared as a carcinogen, may be one way to prevent the formation of carcinogens.

Even though natural food can be carcinogenic, do not avoid fruits and vegetables. Natural food can also contain anti-cancer ingredients. For example diets high in broccoli, cauliflower and cabbage can help fight off cancer. The greatest risk of cancer cited in the article in *American health* was from not eating enough vegetables. The risk is 700 in 1,000.

Of the three risks, the danger of cancer from chemicals added to our food is insignificant if compared to the danger of cancer from naturally occurring substances in our food. The greatest risk of diet caused cancer is from not eating the fruit and vegetables in the first place.

What You Know...

Lowering cholesterol increases life expectancy

...that is not so

A trip through your favorite supermarket must convince you that lowering cholesterol is important. Food after food is touted as cholesterol free. Other foods are touted as effective in lowering cholesterol. Fat free and cholesterol free ice cream substitutes are now sold. Cereals are marketed as "heart-wise" because they contain no cholesterol.

TV and radio programs tell us about diets that will lower cholesterol. Magazine articles tell us how to lower cholesterol. Food columns feature recipes to lower cholesterol.

Pamphlets passed out at hospitals, shopping malls, and doctors' offices explain how to lower cholesterol. Free or low cost cholesterol screenings are offered.

The trendy isle of Sausalito, California declares itself a cholesterol free zone.

Every so often a scientific study is announced. "Proof positive lowering cholesterol protects from heart attacks," declares the researcher when announcing the results of his study. Headlines spread the good news. The results are reviewed by the appropriate medical authorities. Controversies over the studies develop and so another study is launched.

Drug companies produce cholesterol lowering drugs. Surgeons remove part of the intestine to cause a lowering of cholesterol. New studies appear. New headlines announce that lowering cholesterol works. Controversy develops again.

The headlines keep proclaiming that lowering cholesterol will save your life, but new studies are funded because doubts keep appearing. Even though the doubters are published in prestigious journals like *Lancet, Annals of Internal Medicine* and the *Journal of the American Medical Association*, we laypeople get little hint of the controversy. Everything we hear pushes the benefit of lowering cholesterol.

Cholesterol is essential for life. The body uses it to form cell membranes, certain hormones and other important chemicals. Although some cholesterol comes from food, the liver manufactures most cholesterol in the body. Cholesterol is found throughout the body. Only a small percentage circulates in the blood.

In the blood, cholesterol is found in packages called lipoproteins. These are combinations of cholesterol, proteins and fats. One type of lipoprotein, called lipoprotein (LDL) deposits cholesterol on artery walls, a second type, called High Density Lipoprotein (HDL) carries the deposited cholesterol back to the liver for disposal. A third lipoprotein, called very low density lipoprotein (VLDL) carries fats called Triglycerides.

The role of cholesterol in heart disease is not clear. It does build up in arteries like sludge in a pipe. The build up is associated with narrowing the opening in the artery and restricting the flow of blood. One theory is the body fills in cracks in artery walls by trowelling cholesterol over the injuries. These fat deposits called plaques can block off an artery and cause a heart attack. Statistics do show a correlation between heart attacks and high cholesterol levels. So why is there a controversy over lowering cholesterol?

One of the reasons is based on the methods used to lower cholesterol. Early clinical trials used Clofibrate, Estrogen and Dextrothyroxine. These drugs did more harm then good. The Coronary Drug Project Research Group terminated some tests because the treated group experienced higher mortality then the placebo treated group.[7] Recent tests have used diet, the drug Mevacor, niacin and surgical intestinal bypass to lower cholesterol. These are not without side effects. Few doctors would recommend a surgical bypass to reduce an elevated cholesterol level, except in the most extreme cases. Even the extreme diets needed to lower cholesterol have dangerous side effects. Both niacin and Mevacor have caused liver problems in a percentage of those treated with these drugs.

In all the clinical tests reported by enthusiastic laboratories, one fact stands out. Even though deaths from heart related causes fell, the over all deaths stayed high. Deaths from other causes replaced deaths from heart attacks.

Most surveys of clinical trials have shown no drop in overall mortality, even though a drop in deaths from coronary artery disease did occur. A survey by Ingar Holme, Ph.D.[8] on the effects of cholesterol reduction on mortality and coronary heart disease did show some reduction in total mortality if the cholesterol was lowered 8-9%. However this study dropped out the results of clinical trials that resulted in higher death rates among subjects lowering cholesterol. (Some studies used drugs to lower cholesterol that caused more deaths than the cholesterol would have caused. Those being treated to lower cholesterol died more quickly than the untreated control group.) The study also included tests on groups that already suffered from coronary artery heart disease (CHD). These groups should benefit more from lowering cholesterol than the general population. That is because lowering cholesterol does lower the incidence of CHD which is the greatest risk among a group suffering from CHD. For the general population, however, deaths from other causes are also significant. After taking these factors into consideration, even his survey seems to be negative for any lowering of overall mortality by lowering cholesterol.

At this time we should detour and discuss the importance of theory in science. Facts hang on a theory like lights on a Christmas tree. If there is no theory, then facts are just left on the floor, awaiting the erection of the tree. Most of science consists of experiments designed to test and refine the theory.

These researchers studying cholesterol had a theory. The theory connected heart disease with a build up of cholesterol. The reduction in deaths from heart related causes fit into the theory. The offsetting increase in deaths; from suicide, one car accidents, and violence did not fit into the theory. (The incidence of cancer, strokes and gallstones also rose as cholesterol went down.) These were ignored. Nevertheless, many studies showed this offsetting increase of deaths from causes that "could not be related to the test".

Diet and mood are related. Many overweight people have found the need to binge on food during a period of depression. Some foods, such as coffee or chocolate are practically addicting to some people. A person deprived of chocolate may become depressed. People subject to this effect jokingly call themselves chocoholics. Low fat diets may also cause depression. Even author Annmarie Colbin admitted "many people on long term very low fat diets are notably irritable, fidgety, nervous and depressed." [9] One of the foremost advocates of low fat diets, Nathan Pritikin committed suicide after following a low fat diet for many years. The Pritikin diet is very successful at lowering cholesterol. His followers have not associated his suicide with his diet.

Cholesterol is a precursor of hormones in the body. The body uses cholesterol to manufacture certain hormones. Diet and chemicals that lower cholesterol also lower the ultimate hormone level. This effect may have caused some of the deaths that occurred during the studies. Depression can certainly be implicated in suicide, one car accidents and violent deaths. Now science has a theory on which to hang these once considered unrelated deaths. The over all death rate during these clinical trials has never gone down. Only the deaths from heart related causes have gone down. (Drug manufacturers hope that the newest drug, pravastatin will lower overall deaths. If it does, it will be the first to do so.)

Because the overall death rate has consistently remained level, with deaths from alternative causes replacing deaths from

heart disease during the clinical trials, the idea that lowering cholesterol will increase life expectancy for people not at high risk
because of previous CHD, is clearly unproven at today's level of
knowledge. Any life prolonging effects of cholesterol lowering
treatment are difficult to detect, and require a life time of faithful
adherence to diet and drugs. By foregoing the pleasures of ice cream,
roast beef and eggs, in favor of bean sprouts, brussel sprouts and
watercress, you may not live any longer, but it will seem longer.

What You Know...

Sir Alexander Fleming proved Penicillin could cure disease in people

...that is not so.

The noble prize for the discovery of penicillin was given jointly to Sir Alexander Fleming, Professor Ernest Chain, and Sir Howard Florey. Most people are familiar with the name of Sir Alexander Fleming in association with the discovery of penicillin, but what of the other two? What did they have to do with the discovery of penicillin?

The story of penicillin has some startling coincidences and accidents that could lead a superstitious reader to believe an unseen hand led to the discovery.

It is likely that few researchers would have noticed the peculiar petri dish that started off the chain of accidents. Fleming was uniquely prepared to observe the accidentally contaminated dish. Years before the incident that led to the discovery of penicillin, Fleming had done work with human tears. He discovered that tears, and other body fluids were powerful germ killers. The eye is exposed to a multitude of germs, but resists infection because of a property called lysis. Fleming had discovered lysozyme. He frequently demonstrated lysozyme by drawing a tear from his eye and dropping it into a solution made cloudy by scrapping germs off a culture plate and mixing them into the solution. When his tears were added the solution cleared.

On the fateful day he first noticed penicillin, Fleming was discarding a group of dishes that had been accidentally contaminated. One spoiled dish caught his attention. There was a patch of mold growing in a colony of staphylococci. Surrounding the mold was a clear moat between the mold and the staphylococci. It is likely that most researchers would have discarded that dish with the others. Fleming, however had a mind prepared to notice the clear moat around the mold. He decided to investigate. He found that staphylococci, streptococci, the bacilli of diphtheria, and anthrax would not grow close to the mold. He used it to treat boils and other surface infections, but found it not as good as treatments already available. Furthermore it lost its potency quickly. Fleming wrote up a report and penicillin reverted to a laboratory curiosity for ten more years.

Some years before, Paul Ehrlich had developed a drug to cure syphilis. The drug salvarsan was used to kill a selected germ inside the body. Despite this predecessor drug, Fleming did not try penicillin internally.

The experimental climate changed after sulfanilamide was used to cure child bed fever. The story of sulfanilamide has almost as many peculiarities as the story of penicillin. It was first synthesized by an Austrian student, Paul Gelmo , as a student project at the Vienna institute of technology. I. G. Farben used it as a dye. One of their bacteriologists experimented with dyes as germicides. When his own daughter developed blood poisoning, he tested it on her. She was dying. It cured her. Farben patented the drug, but the patent was overthrown because Gelmo had done the original work. Sulfanilamide became available to chemists all over the world, and the search for drugs that could be used like sulfa and salvarsan became popular. Many years later Gelmo was found working in an obscure printing firm. He was unaware of the momentous importance of the discovery he had made 38 years before.

The advent of sulfanilamide had changed the outlook of scientists all over the world. Now science was searching for substances that could operate internally, in a manner similar to sulfanilamide and salvarsan. That was the kind of thing Howard Florey, the Australian born professor of pathology at Oxford University, was seeking. Professor Florey was interested in lysozyme, Fleming's original discovery. He had purified it and was experimenting with it. He assigned his research assistant, Ernest Chain the task of searching for substances with similar properties of dissolving germs. Chain was a brilliant biochemist who had escaped from Hitler's Germany.

Chain had never heard of penicillin until he found Fleming's paper in the library. The report which had seemed to close out research on penicillin had some factors which drew special attention to a biochemist like Chain. Fleming had become discouraged because penicillin lost its potency so quickly. To Chain this was an especially intriguing characteristic. Also, the kinds of germs it was effective against were the causes of serious illness. Chain decided to investigate penicillin. In another piece of luck, the original Fleming molds from eleven years before, were still available.

Supported by Professor Florey, and with a team of able chemists, Chain grew the mold in whatever equipment he could obtain in war torn Britain. They used dog baths, milk churns, bed pans, and milk bottles. The team was able to obtain a tiny amount of true penicillin. They painfully accumulated enough for a clinical test.

In another of the Chain of coincidences, they did not test penicillin in guinea pigs. If they had, we might never have obtained penicillin, because penicillin is fatal to guinea pigs.[10] Instead, penicillin was tested on a dying policeman. He rallied and improved. Then their supply of penicillin ran out and he died.

Because of the war shortages, Britain could not produce penicillin. Professor Florey, together with a chemist who had helped produce the laboratory supplies, went to the United States, where the technology to mass produce penicillin was developed.

When the story of penicillin was sought by reporters after the war, Fleming cooperated with the journalists. The very private Professor Florey, and the even more private Ernest Chain refused interviews. Since all the stories discussed Fleming, and none discussed the other two, the full credit has gone to Fleming. The even greater work of Florey and Chain has fallen out of the public eye.

Scientists do not like to talk of luck and coincidence. The chain of events that led to penicillin seems like luck or coincidence. In any case the proof that penicillin can cure disease in humans was not done by Fleming.

What You Know...

Milk is good for ulcers

...that is not so

The traditional diet of milk and cream to soothe an ulcer has been abandoned. Ulcers are treated with drugs that stop acid formation like Tagamet. The newest idea is that ulcers are caused by bacteria. Research is proceeding to develop drugs to stop infection.

What You Know...

Banning DDT saved lives

...that is not so

Even when the ban was passed, the justification was not saving human lives. DDT was accused of causing the shells of birds to be formed too thin to properly protect the eggs. The endangered birds were the beneficiaries, not humans.

Humans however, became the victims of the ban. For example, in Sri Lanka about one and a half million people died of malaria each year, until DDT became widely available. After using DDT a few years the death rate dropped to less than 200 per year. After the ban, the death rate climbed back to exceed a million a year.

Banning DDT did not save lives. It cost lives.

Some things we know from tv ...

The Audi 5000 would suddenly accelerate by itself

...that is not so.

A highly rated TV show, tried and convicted Audi of sudden acceleration. The alleged defect was supposed to have caused a mother to run over and kill her 6 year old child. By the time the show finished the Audi was nearly destroyed.

The United States Government conducted extensive tests and proved that driver error was responsible.[11] When drivers put their foot on the gas pedal instead of the brake the car accelerated. The government reports were too late to save Audi from huge financial losses. A variety of suits have been filed against Audi. One class action suit even claims damage from Audi for loss of resale value caused by the bad publicity. It is unlikely that a suit against CBS would hold up against the free press safeguards for the press, even though the error was a television news magazine show's misrepresentations, and not Audi's design.

What You Know...

Alar is dangerous

...that is not so.

Another TV show attacked the chemical additive Alar. Alar was used to enhance the appearance of apples. The bad publicity caused apple growers to request a ban on Alar, so that the general public could be sure all apples were Alar free. To this date all government studies show Alar is safe. Rats had to ingest the equivalent of 60,000 bottles of apple juice each day to produce cancer.

Part Four

Things You Know About Religion
That Are Not So

What You Know...

The immortal soul that goes to heaven is an idea from the Jewish Bible

...that is not so

The picture of heaven that is commonly presented, has souls of dead people seated at the foot of God, basking in his glory. The idea that a soul arises from the dead body and ascends to heaven to spend eternity there is commonly understood to come from the Bible.

Preachers frighten their congregation with tales of heaven and hell. The idea that we have immortal souls seems to have roots in the Bible.

Scientists have tried to weigh bodies as death occurs but have failed to detect any loss of weight. If there is an immortal soul, it has no weight.

Many motion pictures have been made with a dead man's soul meeting an angel and coming back to Earth to help the living. "Here Comes Mr. Jordan" was made twice. In this charming motion picture, an inexperienced angel pulls the soul of the hero from his body before the hero's time to die. The hero gets an alternate body to use. The comic possibilities are well explored.

Death is so final, so irreversible, that few of us can come to terms with it. There is a certain comfort to the idea that we have an immortal soul. Does this idea come from the Old Testament? The answer is no.

Check a Bible concordance and you will not find the words "immortal soul" together. The Old Testament does not relate any story of anyone dying and going to heaven. Quite the contrary, Solomon, in the book of Ecclesiastes wrote "for that which befalleth the sons of men befalleth beasts; even one thing befalleth them: as the one dieth, so dieth the other: yea they all have one breath: so that a man hath no preeminence above a beast: for all is vanity. All go unto one place; all are of the dust, and all turn to dust again" (Ecclesiastes 3:19-20) he goes on to say "for a living dog is better than a dead lion. For the living know that they shall die: but the dead know not anything". Scripture tells us even David, beloved of God, is dead and in the grave.

The only hope for immortality from the Old Testament is the resurrection and judgment at the end of days. The Bible speaks often of the resurrection. Daniel, chapter 12 verses 1-2 reads, "and at that time shall Michael stand up, the great prince which standeth for the children of thy people: and there shall be a time of trouble, such as never was since there was a nation, even to that same time: And at that time thy people shall be delivered, every one that shall be found written in the book. And many of them that sleep in the dust of the Earth shall awake..." Until then the gist of the Bible implies the dead stay dead and know nothing.

If the immortal soul is not from the Old Testament, where does it come from? The idea of an immortal soul is found in pagan Greek mythology. Charon ferries these shades of the dead across the River Styx and they dwell in Hades. Plato, in the Phaedo wrote "the soul whose inseparable attitude is life will never admit of life's opposite, death. Thus the soul is shown to be immortal, and since immortal, indestructible...do we believe there is such a thing as death? To be sure. And is this anything but the separation of the soul and the body?"

What You Know...

The original sin was eating an apple from the tree of knowledge

...that is not so

Many people seem to know that the symbolic fruit was not identified as an apple, but few realize that the tree was not the tree of knowledge. It is a simple matter to pick up a Bible and read any translation. The fruit was picked from the tree of knowledge of *good and evil*. This is completely different and startlingly wise.

The knowledge of good and evil refers to a moral sense. Proof of this is the next event mentioned in Genesis. Adam and Eve cover up their nakedness. They became ashamed of their nakedness.

I call the story startlingly wise because history has proven that the original sin has been the cause of most of man's strife ever since.

Most wars have been fought by two or more armies each thinking moral right was on its side. People do not usually fight for evil. It is man's moral sense that makes him willing to sacrifice.

Even when greed and envy are the true motivation, the armies must be fed a moral justification. Pizzaro and Cortez exhorted their armies to bring Christianity to the heathen. The crusades were a Christian holy war fought against a Moslem holy war. In modern times, both Great Britain and Argentina claimed right and morality in the Falklands war. Even Saddam Hassein could give a moral justification for annexing Kuwait.

Communism made destitute slaves of millions, but it was originally designed to free these same people from the problems of capitalism. The concept of to each as he needs; from each as he can is attractive. However it only works for ants and bees. Humans need more personal rewards. Everyone is willing to be on the "to each" side, but the "from each" side requires a gun to make it work. Communism is a text book example of morality gone wrong.

When Right To Lifers oppose freedom of choice proponents, both believe morality is on their side. One is saving the life of an innocent baby. The other is saving the rights of a trapped mother. When Palestinian Arabs confront Israelis, both believe right is on their side. Both can point to injustice done to them, and the necessity to right wrongs. When the inquisition tortured heretics, the purpose was to save the soul of the poor victim.

Even that figure of evil incarnate, Adolf Hitler, claimed in his book "Mein Kampf", to have God's support for his program. The German people thought the nazis were; 1. cleansing their nation by expelling non Aryans that the Germans blamed for the recent inflation that had devastated the savings of the thrifty, 2. uniting their nation by annexing areas populated by ethnic Germans such as parts of Czechoslovakia, and 3. righting the injustices of the Treaty of Versaille that Germans saw as punishing them for losing the first world war. Just by not looking, the German people could avoid seeing the horrible crimes committed by the nazi government.

Censors fight to save us from immorality, while freedom of speech is the good promoted by the other side. Both are fighting for their moral sense of right and wrong.

It is probably possible to justify most conflicts by claiming right is on your side. Certainly the most intractable conflicts arise from a clash of sincere righteousness and morality.

Most of us grew up believing that we could judge right from wrong, moral from immoral, justice from injustice. One of mankind's most respected thinkers, Kant, proposed what he called the "Categorical Imperative". This can be thought of as the idea that everyone has an innate moral sense. It is when we look out at nature and see a world that does not conform to our innate moral sense that we become disillusioned. We demand to know how God can permit all the "evil" we see. We turn to religious leaders to find answers, but they have the same misunderstanding of the nature of good and evil as all humankind.

Good cannot exist unless evil exists. They are two sides of the same coin. If the only choice is good, if there can be no choice of evil, then we are only automata. Free will can only be real if there is a choice of evil. If evil did not exist, we would be like a ball thrown to a catcher. "How wonderful I am," thinks the ball. "I go just to the right place." But the ball has no choice. It must go where we throw it. Any free will it thinks it has is an illusion.

This world is characterized by certain factors that our human sense of morality finds repugnant. To live, every creature must eat. As much as we hate to think about it, meat does not grow in plastic wrap. People eat chickens, chickens eat worms, and worms eat people. A vegetarian may try to opt out for moral reasons, but at the end he will be recycled just as all other meat.

Humans extol love. We consider love a high human emotion. Like it or not, we express this ultimate emotion with organs that are part of our excretory system. Could the adjoining of our genitals and our urinary tract — a union of our highest with our lowest functions- be part of the ultimate joke that nature (or God) has played on our high moral sense?

What You Know...

The Immaculate Conception refers to the virgin birth of Jesus

...that is not so

There are three concepts to discuss:
1. Original sin
2. Virgin birth
3. Immaculate conception

Original sin refers to the fall of Adam and Eve because of their disobedience. According to the doctrine of original sin, all humans, even new born babies, are guilty of original sin.

The Virgin Birth, a biblical doctrine, states that Jesus was miraculously begotten by God and born of Mary, who was a virgin. Mary would be guilty of original sin, be she virgin or not, since all human beings are guilty of Adam and Eve's sin.

Virginity does not mean free of original sin. If it did, all females would be immaculately conceived. Sexual relations within marriage are not a sin, and sex in any form is not the sin that is referred to when we speak of original sin.

The Immaculate Conception is a comparatively recent doctrine of the Roman Catholic Church. It states that Mary, mother of Jesus, was born free of original sin. The sin of Adam and Eve applies to all human beings, except Mary.

What You Know...

Christmas is Christ's birthday

...that is not so.

Probably no other subject is filled with more misconceptions than the origin of the holidays. Christmas, for example has a history that goes back deep into pagan days. Many religious Christian groups have forbidden the celebration of Christmas, because of its pagan origin. When the puritans, under Oliver Cromwell came into power in England, Parliament forbid both religious and secular celebrations of Christmas. Puritan colonies in North America also forbade the celebration of Christmas.

Celebration of a holiday on December 25 was done by pagan groups because the sun began its return to northern skies, promising a new spring after the winter. This ancient holiday continued to be celebrated by the Romans and other pre Christian groups until the adoption of Christianity by Rome.

The holly wreath, Yule log, and mistletoe were all part of the pagan sun worship practices.[1] Even the Madonna and child occur as objects of worship as early as Babylon, and in ancient Egypt mother and child statues of gods have been found.

The early Christians did not celebrate Christmas. It was at least three hundred years after Christ died that the celebration of Christmas became common among Christians.[2]

The date of Christ's birth is not known. However internal evidence of the events described in the Bible indicate that Christ was not born in December. For example, because of weather conditions, the sheep were not out in the fields at night as late as December. The tax collections that brought Mary and Joseph to Jerusalem, were not done in December. These kinds of things have made scholars sure that December was not the month of Christ's birth.

Just as Christmas has an ancient history that predates Christianity, so do other holidays. St. Valentine's day sounds like a Christian holiday. It is named after a saint. However it has roots in a pagan holiday called "Lupercalia", which was celebrated on the evening of February 14th, and the next day. (Many ancient people started holidays on sundown of the previous day.) On this day the names of young women were drawn at random by the young men for a kind of mock betrothal.

The symbol of the heart derives from a kind of pun. The earliest celebration of the day dedicated the day to honor Baal, an ancient God. The word for heart in their language was bal. Because the sound is so similar, the heart became a symbol for the day. The God Baal was known as Nimrod and as Osiris by different nations. Nimrod as a boy was sometimes called Cupid, which means "desire", because his mother desired him, and later wed him. Cupid is depicted as a winged boy armed with a bow and arrow. He is naked and blind. His arrows strike the heart and cause love to arise. In Rome Cupid was called Eros.

Many of the customs and symbols such as hearts, cupids, and lovers uniting, predate Christianity. St. Valentine's day, like Christmas is an ancient pagan holiday.

What about Easter? By now the reader has probably become suspicious. What do Easter eggs, bunnies, and hot cross buns have to do with the resurrection? The answer is, these also are ancient prechristian symbols, used in fertility rites. The celebration of the resurrection, which seems so central to Christianity, actually had a counterpart in paganism. At the same season, in ancient Syria, a holiday celebrated the dead and risen Adonis.[3]

The early Christian church celebrated none of these holidays. The masses of people, however, continued to enjoy the ancient holidays. As a way to unify and solidify the masses with the church, the root stock of ancient holidays was used as a base for new Christianized holidays. In this way, the masses could continue to celebrate holidays, but the church tried to change the nature of the holidays to make them acceptable. The prevalence of bunnies and colored eggs, holly wreaths, mistletoe, and trees, as well as hearts indicates how well the Christianization succeeded.

Part Five

Some Other Things You Know, That Are Not So.

What You Know...

55 saves lives

...that is not so.

The 55 mile per hour speed limit was first instituted as a fuel economy measure. When the gas crises ended, the speed limit was retained because it was purported to save lives. In 1987 Congress allowed the speed limit to be raised on certain interstate roads to 65 miles per hour. Initial published reports claim that raising the speed limit has resulted in higher traffic death rates. This author contends that an analysis of the same data shows that the 65 mph limit has not cost lives. Furthermore, the 55 mile per hour speed limit not only failed to save lives, it actually cost lives.

Unrealistic low speed limits have cost lives through two important effects. First, there are fewer incentives to use safer, limited access highways. Second, there is an increase in speed variance between the slowest and fastest drivers. When we look at the statistics that resulted after the majority of the states raised their speed limit we find both effects. We find that the states that raised their speed limit had better results than the states that kept the 55 mph speed limit. Even more significantly, the states that had the greatest increase in deaths on their interstates because of increased use, had the greatest savings in deaths overall.

If you believe 55 saves lives, you have plenty of company. The national highway traffic safety administration, quoted by the national safety council[1], in a report to Congress, stated "In the first 28 states that raised the speed limit, rural interstate fatalities increased 18 percent during June-December, 1987 versus 1986". It also stated "eight states (Arizona, California, New Mexico, North Carolina, Ohio, Tennessee, Texas, and Utah) accounted for 71 per cent of the total 1987 increase in rural interstate fatalities in those states that raised their interstate speed limit."

Here the emphasis is placed on the deaths that occurred on the roads that were involved in the higher speed limit and not the overall state results. This may be an error. If the total deaths in the eight states are compared 1986 versus 1988 the result is startling. The eight states had 15,152 total traffic deaths in 1986[2]. The total fell to 15,105 in 1988. This becomes more startling when compared with the entire United States' results for the same period. The deaths in the United States rose from 48,300 to 49,000[3] for the same two years.

Of the eight states singled out as special problems, only one (Ohio)[4] had an increase in death rate per 100,000,000 vehicle miles. By contrast three states, (Delaware, New York and Hawaii)[5], that retained the 55 mph had an increase in the 100,000,000 vehicle miles' death rate. Furthermore, in contrast to the lower total deaths of the eight states discussed above that raised the speed limit, the states that still have the 55 mph limit experienced a rise in total deaths, from 7,492 in 1986 to 7,732 in 1988[6].

1986 was used as the last full year with 55 mph speed limit for all states. 1988 is the first full year for the 65 mph limit for most states that raised the limit. Alaska, Georgia and Virginia raised the speed limit to 65 mph during 1988[7].

Just what is going on here? Why did the number of deaths on 65 mph interstates rise, while total deaths in some of these same states fell? Note that total deaths in the conservative states rose? States that raised the speed limit experienced a decline in total traffic deaths. States that kept the low speed limit experienced an increase in total traffic deaths.

Although I believe the comparison is most meaningful if the eight states cited in the NHTSA report are compared with the

119

states that retained 55 mph as their speed limit, the comparison of all states is also interesting. As I stated above, the states that did not raise the speed limit had an increase in total deaths, from 7,492 in 1986 to 7,732 in 1988. This is an increase of 3.2 per cent. The states that raised their speed limit to 65 mph had an increase of less than 1.2 per cent. Furthermore, only five of these states had an increase in deaths per 100,000,000 vehicle miles. 3 out of nine of the states that kept 55 mph had an increase in the per 100,000,000 vehicle miles death rate, as did the District of Columbia, which also kept the 55 mph limit[8]. If the proportions were the same, twelve or thirteen states with the 65 mph limit would have experienced a rise in per vehicle miles death rate, instead of just five states.

The reader may question why a comparison of the eight states mentioned in the NHTSA report to the states that kept 55 mph as the speed limit, instead of comparing all states that raised the speed limit, is more meaningful. The reason is if a state does not have a higher death rate on the 65 mph interstates, there is no reason to attribute deaths on other roads to the 65 mph limit. The eight states that have a higher death rate on the 65 mph roads are the states that could blame the excess deaths on the 65 mph speed limit. They could also credit the lower traffic deaths to the higher speed limit if, for example, the higher speed limit diverted traffic from more dangerous to less dangerous roads.

Another factor is the gradual increase in total traffic deaths in the nation, the year the speed limit was raised. The eight states in question actually lowered total traffic deaths, against the trend, and this is especially significant.

An important factor is vehicle miles traveled increased 8.4 per cent on rural interstates in the states that raised the speed limit, but there was only a 5.2 per cent increase in those states that kept 55 mph limit[9]. The increase had the effect of increasing fatalities on rural interstates, but it also had the effect of reducing fatalities on the roads that diverted traffic to the interstate. These rural interstates are among the safest roads in the country. Diverting traffic to them should reduce deaths overall.

Let us expand this concept to other limited access roads. Drivers traveling between Philadelphia, Pa. and Atlantic City, NJ. Have a choice of three routes. They can use the White Horse Pike, the Black Horse Pike, or the Atlantic City expressway. The White Horse Pike and, to a lesser extent the Black Horse Pike are far more dangerous than the expressway. Both roads go through local towns, traffic lights and pedestrians crossings. Left turns can be made from the main road. Cross streets and poorly engineered curves add to the risk. By contrast, the expressway is a modern, safe, limited access highway. There are no crossroads, no traffic lights, no pedestrians, no left turns, and the curves are engineered for safety. The expressway has a toll of $1.25. The other roads are free. The speed limit is 55 mph on the expressway. Both the White Horse and Black Horse Pikes have 55 mph speed limits on portions of their route and less on other portions. If the expressway allowed 65 mph there would be greater incentive to use it. Any traffic diverted to the expressway is a safety plus.

The same situation is repeated all over the country. Old, hazardous routes parallel modern safe limited access highways. Yet in many areas the hazardous route has the same 55 mph speed limit as the safer road.

There are other factors to account for the better safety record of states with 65 mph limits. A study done for the AAA foundation for traffic safety by Nicholas J. Garber And Ravi Gadireau, both of the School of Engineering at the University of Virginia, concluded that a speed limit close to the design speed of the roadway is safer than a speed limit set too low[10]. The study points out that speed variance increases accident rates, and speed variance is less when posted speeds are 5 to 10 mph less than design speed. A speed limit set too low increases speed variance[11]. This is because some drivers will obey the speed limit and others will drive at speeds close to the design speed of the road. A low speed limit increases the speed variance between these different types of drivers. The report also states that accident rates on a highway do not necessarily increase with increase in average speed[12].

In conclusion, raising the speed limit to 65 mph on interstates did not cost lives. The higher speed limit diverts traffic from more dangerous to less dangerous roads. The higher speed limit raised the driving speed of less aggressive drivers to a speed that is closer to the speed of the faster drivers, thus narrowing the dangerous speed variance. The combined effect is less traffic deaths then would otherwise occur. Both expert theories such as the AAA foundation study and actual results since the limited 65 mph speed limit became available show that 55 does not save lives. It costs lives.

What You Know...

Life insurance won't pay if the insured commits suicide

...that is not so.

Numerous murder mysteries and dramas have used a plot device in which a death by suicide was disguised because the life insurance will not pay for death by suicide. All life insurance policies have a suicide clause. This clause states that the policy will pay for death by suicide if the insured has the good grace to wait two years after the policy has been issued before committing suicide. Only if the insured was really trying to defraud the insurance company by purchasing the policy and shortly thereafter committing suicide can the insurance company refuse the claim.

What You Know...

You can't convict a murderer without the body of the victim (corpus delicti)

...that is not so.

The phrase "corpus delicti" is often used as if it means the "victim's body". Many plots claim the murderer will be freed because the body cannot be found. "Corpus delicti" means the "body of the crime." It is not referring to the victim. It is referring to the establishment of a crime. The "corpus delicti" can be established by all the circumstances that add up to proving a crime has been committed. Many murderers have been convicted without a body being found.

What You Know...

Nursery rhymes were written for children

...that is not so

According to the Oxford dictionary of nursery rhymes, most nursery rhymes written before 1800 were never intended for children. Some of the rhymes were refrains from bawdy folk songs. Others were based on proverbs, prayers, distortions of Shakespeare's sonnets or popular street games. The purpose of many of the rhymes was social or political satire or to mock religious practices. Some of the rhymes originated as tavern limericks.

Although many of the rhymes were cleaned up during Victorian times, observers still question the fitness of many rhymes for children. However, even the rhymes and stories that were written for children are as questionable as the old rhymes written for adults that are now cleaned up.

An example of these concerns is the giant's cannibalistic statement from Jack and the Bean Stalk.

> fee, fi, fo, fum,
> I smell the blood of an Englishman!
> be he 'live or be he dead
> I'll grind his bones to make my bread!

Hansel and Gretel is another favorite that was written for children. It features the threat of roasting and eating the pair of children, and ends with a roasted villainess.

Typical of the nursery rhymes originally aimed for adult satire is "Humpty Dumpty".

> Humpty Dumpty sat on a wall,
> Humpty Dumpty had a great fall,
> all the king's horses,
> and all the king's men,
> couldn't put Humpty together again.

This is dated about 500 years old, and believed to mock a noble-man who fell out of favor with King Richard lll. The rhyme spread to Europe where the lead character became "wirgele-wargele in Germany, Boule, Boule in France, and Thille Lille in Sweden."

Today, a "Humpty Dumpty" is a short, clumsy and rotund person, male or female.

"Jack and Jill" is another political satire.

> Jack and Jill went up the hill
> to fetch a pail of water
> Jack fell down and broke his crown,
> and Jill came tumbling after.

Early versions refer to two boys, Jack and Gill. They are identified as Cardinal Wolsey and Bishop Tarbes. The two traveled back and forth attempting to negotiate a peace between France and the Hapsburgs. They failed and war erupted. Wolsey then commit-ted British troops to assist the Hapsburgs. The war provoked wide-spread resentment among the British, and the rhyme parodied his uphill peace efforts that finally failed.

In New England, Mother Goose is frequently identified as a Boston widow named Elizabeth Goose. She was the stepmother of ten children and birth mother of six children. Allegedly, her son-in-law, Thomas Fleet published a volume of nursery rhymes. Al-though Elizabeth Goose and Thomas Fleet are real people, no copy of the book has ever been found. Most authorities believe the origi-nal Mother Goose was Charles Perrault.

In 1696 Charles Perrault published in France a book en-titled "Mere L'oye Tales". This book included eight tales. These tales, such as Sleeping Beauty, Puss In Boots, and Cinderella were clearly meant for children, but as in Hansel and Gretel and Jack and the Bean Stalk some scenes include events that are not acceptable to modern parents. Our English version of Little Red Riding Hood usually omits the grotesque climax of the older versions. In "Little Red Riding Hood" the wolf swallowed the little girl's grandmother. A passing hunter rescued her. The hunter slashes open the wolf and pulls her out still alive. Other stories in the book were "The Fairy,""Riquet With The Tuft," "Little Thum," and "Blue Beard".

The tradition of gory stories for children continued with the very grim stories by the Brothers Grimm. It would be difficult to claim that the cannibalism of "Hansel and Gretel" is more suitable for children than the bawdy satires of the earlier nursery rhymes.

Sensitive parents trying to insulate their children from war and violence will have just as much difficulty with modern children's stories. The acts of violence committed in cartoons presented on Saturday morning TVs are the equal of any previous cohort of children's tales.

Because so many of the nursery rhymes that were originally adult satires are now cleaned and made suitable for children, while stories written directly for children deal in cannibalism, violence and other taboos, the modern parent may find traditional children's literature unsuitable. A brief survey of school readers shows modern books are little improved. One school book describes the Egyptian embalming practice, including removing the brain from the body by drawing it out through the nose. Another book aimed at early readers encourages the child to practice occult rituals practiced by witches, warlocks and devil worshippers.

The amazing thing is the children raised under all these violent and superstitious ideas grow up normal... Or do they?

What You Know...

The lion's share is the largest portion.

...that is not so.

This book is about things that everyone knows, that are not so. The English language, however is a democratic language without official arbiters. If everyone is wrong about a meaning, then communication becomes impossible. Today, only a few know the meaning of the expression "the lion's share". If you were to use it correctly, only a few readers would understand the irony of the expression. To everyone else you would be pedantic. At some future time, the expression will have only the weak meaning so many now accept.

The expression comes from a fable of Aesop, called "The Lion's Share". In the fable, the lion, the fox, the jackal, and the wolf hunt and kill a stag. The question arose of how the spoil should be divided. "Quarter me this stag," roared the lion. The other animals skinned it and cut it into four parts. Then the lion took his stand in front of the carcass and said, "the first quarter is for me as king of beasts. The second is mine as arbiter. A third part is mine for my part in the chase. And as to the last, I should like to see which of you will dare to lay a paw on it."

The others slunk away, but the fox whispered, "You may share the labors of the great, but you will not share the spoil."

Thus the meaning of "the lion's share," is one hundred per cent, or all. It means nothing less.

What You Know...

Trees do not cause pollution

...that is not so.

When former President Reagan said that even trees cause pollution, he became the butt of jokes that has lasted for years. Some years after the remark, in 1990, a television program (Crossfire on CNN) broadcast another poke at the former President for that "ridiculous comment".

Planting trees is regarded as a fine way to fight air pollution, and I do endorse planting trees. Yet the President was correct in his statement, and the many commentators were ignorant of the basis for his statement.

Trees do cause pollution!

The National Institute for Occupational Safety and Health published a list of suspected carcinogens in 1976. Anyone who puts one of these suspected carcinogens into the atmosphere would rightly be called a polluter. On that list are the terpenes. In fact terpenes have been selected by the EPA as a high priority pollutant. Terpenes have been identified as coming from trees and other vegetation by a variety of researchers and terpenes constitute a major part of the smoky haze that forms over many forests.

There are many other chemicals emitted by trees that would be called pollutants if emitted by people. Some of these are emitted during naturally occurring forest fires and others by natural decay, rotting leaves, etc. Some are suspected carcinogens. Among these chemicals are tannin, benzo(a)pyrene, pyrrolizidine alkaloids and diterpene esters, all of which have been reported as carcinogenic by one or more researcher.

The many commentators who had a good laugh at the expense of the former President owe him an apology.

What You Know...

Up is always the opposite of down
...that is not so

Slow up, slow down. Burn up, burn down.

What You Know...

John Kennedy was the first president of Irish ancestry

...that is not so

He was the first Catholic president. Fifteen presidents have Irish ancestry (including President Clinton).

What You Know...

St Patrick was Irish
...that is not so

St Patrick was Born in Wales.

What You Know...

King Canute thought he could command the tide to recede

...that is not so

It was not King Canute that thought he could command the tides, it was his courtiers. The king took them to the shore to show them that they were wrong. King Canute should be the hero of the story, instead of the object of derision.

What You Know...

The ugly American was an embarrassment to the United States

...that is not so

Read the book. He was actually the hero of the book.

What You Know...

Uncle Tom was an "uncle Tom"

...that is not so

Read the book. He died rather than betray his friends.

And some things you saw...

Bambi's mother die in the snow

The knife slashing Janet Leigh in the shower scene from Psycho

... That never were shown on the screen

Or some things you heard....

Tarzan saying, "me Tarzan, you Jane" (by the way, in the book by Edgar Rice Burroughs, Tarzan was quite well spoken)

Humphry Bogart saying, "Play it again, Sam".

...that were never said in the films.

What You Know...

Eskimos used to live in igloos made of snow and ice

...that is not so.

The word for building is igloo. It is used for houses of Earth and wood. Snow houses are sometimes built for emergency use while out hunting or traveling on the trail, but are not permanent dwellings.[13]

Some other popular misconceptions about Alaska are:

"The further north you go the colder it gets".

The extreme arctic region is warmed by the ocean. Inland at the low regions, it is much colder than Point Barrow

"Alaska is a frigid land of ice and snow".

Fairbanks sometimes reaches 100 degrees in the shade. Virginia has more average snowfall than large parts of Alaska. Parts of Alaska have luxuriant vegetation and mild climate.

"Glaciers form in extreme cold".

Glaciers form where precipitation is heavy. In Alaska glaciers are found in warmer regions.

What You Know...

Most rape victims are women

...that is not so

Because of the feelings of shame and degradation that fall on the victim of rape, many rapes go unreported. Women's groups have formed to support female victims and encourage them to assist in prosecution of the rapists. Courts have changed procedures to make it easier for the rape victim to testify.

Consciousness has been raised. On some college campuses all men have been called potential rapists. Numerous books and articles keep the problem in the public eye.

Government statistics report the number of women raped each year. The statistical abstract reports 91,522 rapes plus 15,068 attempted rapes in 1991, all female victims. In 1995 the estimate of rapes was raised to 170,000. Government statistics never include males. Yet men are raped.

Homosexual rape is rarely in the public mind. One of the classic movies "Deliverance" featured a homosexual rape scene. This was deleted and a less powerful scene was substituted when the movie was released to TV. If you have never seen this great movie, and you rent it from a video rental, be sure to get the original theater version.

Rape is the sexual penetration of an unwilling person. Homosexual rape of a man can and does happen. The first survey of rapes of males found about 30,000 men admitted they had been raped. Rape of a man is an assault on his very essence, his masculinity. Many men believe that the shame of a man who has been raped is even worse than the shame of a woman. The number of

135

men raped may be far higher then 30,000 male victims. The estimate did not include the prison population.

Rape in prison is widespread. For some men the fear of prison rape is greater than fear of loss of freedom. During the watergate investigation of President Nixon, one of Nixon's attorneys, John Dean, said this was the fear that motivated him to betray his President.

It was also in that era that a protester against the Vietnam war named Stephen Donaldson was jailed. He was beaten savagely and gang raped 50 times in a Washington D.C. Jail. When he was released he started a war of his own, against the secret epidemic of homosexual rape in prison. He is now President of Stop Prison Rape, the only national group focused solely on the problem.

After studying the problem for decades, he estimates there are 250,000 assaults each year in prisons throughout America.[14] 250,000 rapes in prison and 30,000 rapes in the general population adds up to 280,000 rapes against men. The female rapes add up to less than 200,000. Based on Mr. Donaldson's authoritative estimate, the incidence of rapes against males is far higher than the incidence of rape against females. Once again, what you know, "most rape victims are women" is not so.

Notes to part one

1 SLEEPWALKERS, ARTHUR KOESTLER, MACMILLON CO. 1959 P490

2 ARISTOTLE, GALILEO, AND THE TOWER OF PISA LANE COOPER, 1935 p29 NOT ONLY DOES COOPER, IN THIS WELL RESEARCHED BOOK, PROVE CORESSIO WAS THE EXPERIMENTER, HE ALSO FURNISHES MANY FORERUNNERS WHO CORRECTLY DESCRIBED THE EFFECT OF WEIGHT ON FALLING BODIES LONG BEFORE GALILEO.

3 MOST BIOGRAPHERS TELL THIS INCIDENT. THE ARCHIVES OF THE WESTINGHOUSE COMPANY COULD NOT VERIFY OR DENY THE INCIDENT.

4 THE POPULATION BOMB, EHRLICH

5 THE END OF AFFLUENCE 1974 BALLANTINE BOOKS P 191

6 THE RUSSIAN REVOLUTION ALAN MOOREHEAD 1958 HARPER AND ROW P 51

7 FRANK VANDERLIP "FARM BOY TO FINANCIER" SATURDAY EVENING POST FEB. 9, 1935

8 "THE POWERS OF FINANCIAL CAPITALISM HAD ANOTHER FAR REACHING AIM, NOTHING LESS THAN TO CREATE A WORLD SYSTEM OF FINANCIAL CONTROL IN PRIVATE HANDS, ABLE TO DOMINATE THE POLITICAL SYSTEM OF EACH COUNTRY, AND THE ECONOMY OF THE WORLD AS A WHOLE. THE SYSTEM WAS TO BE CONTROLLED IN FEUDALIST FASHION BY THE CENTRAL BANKS OF THE WORLD ACTING IN CONCERT, BY SECRET AGREEMENTS ARRIVED AT IN FREQUENT MEETINGS AND CONFERENCES." CARROL QUIGLEY, TRAGEDY AND HOPE NY MACMILLAN CO. 1966 P324. PROFESSOR QUIGLY WAS SYMPATHETIC TO THE GROUPS AIMS AND WAS PRIVY TO THE GROUPS PAPERS. THIS ASTONISHING BOOK REVEALS MANY SECRETS.

9 MUCH OF THIS MATERIAL WAS EXTRACTED FROM "BUFFALO BILL, THE NOBLEST WHITESKIN, JOHN BURKE 1973. OTHER MATERIEL WAS FOUND AT THE BUFFALO BILL MUSEUM, CODY WYOMING.

Notes to part two

1 FROM QUARK TO QUASER, NOTES ON THE SCALE OF THE UNIVERSE, PETER CADOGAN, CAMBRIDGE UNIVERSITY PRESS 1985 P177

2 MOST WRITERS PREFER TO SAY THERE IS NO CENTER, INSTEAD OF THE EQUALLY TRUE STATEMENT THAT EVERY POINT IS THE CENTER.

3 FROM QUARK TO QUASAR P176

4 THE NATURE OF REALITY, RICHARD MORRIS, MCGRAW-HILL, 1987 P202.

5 MEASUREMENTS OF SEDIMENT YIELD IN WESTERN UNITED STATES SHOW THE DENUDATION RATE IS CONSIDERABLY LESS THAN THE UPLIFT RATE IN MANY OROGANIC BELTS. P241 CAMBRIDGE ENCYCLOPEDIA OF EARTH SCIENCES 1981 PRENTICE HALL CANADA

6 CREATIONISTS, ANXIOUS TO PROVE THE WORLD WAS YOUNG, SEIZED ON THE SHALLOW SEDIMENTS AS PROOF THAT THE OCEANS WERE ONLY A FEW THOUSAND YEARS OLD

7 REUTERS OCT. 16, 1991

8 NATIONAL GEOGRAPHIC, FEB. 1994

9 ARNOLD HEIM AND AUGUST GAUSSER, THE THRONE OF THE GODS, AN ACCOUNT OF THE FIRST SWISS EXPEDITION TO THE HIMALOYAS, 1939 P. 218

10 H DE TERRA AND T.T. PATTERSON, STUDIES ON THE ICE AGE IN INDIA AND ASSOCIATED HUMAN CULTURES, 1939.

11 DISCOVER MAGAZINE APRIL 1989 P 36FF

12 MOST WRITERS ON RELATIVITY DISCUSS THIS TIME DILATION EFFECT. A NON-TECHNICAL DISCUSSION CAN BE FOUND IN "THE NATURE OF REAL-ITY" WILLIAM MORRIS PhD. MCGRAW-HILL 1987 P44

13 THE NATURE OF REALITY, RICHARD MORRIS PhD. P73

14 EINSTEIN'S THEORY OF RELATIVITY. MAX BORN. ENGLISH TRANSLA-TION, PUBLISHED BY DOVER PUBLICATIONS 1965 P 345

15 AT ONE POINT DURING HIS CALCULATIONS, EINSTEIN FOUND THE SO-LUTION TO HIS MATHEMATICS PRODUCED AN EXPANDING UNIVERSE. EINSTEIN ARTIFICIALLY INJECTED A NEW CONSTANT INTO THE FORMULA TO OFFSET THE EXPANDING UNIVERSE. LATER, HE CALLED THIS ARTIFICIAL CONSTANT THE GREATEST MISTAKE OF HIS CAREER.

16 ALTHOUGH A COLLISION WITH A COMET IS BELIEVED TO BE THE CAUSE OF THE EXTINCTION OF THE DINOSAURS, THE COMPLEX PATTERN IN WHICH LIFE DIED OUT ON LAND AND SEA PROBABLY TOOK A FEW THOUSAND OR MAYBE FIFTY THOUSAND YEARS TO PLAY OUT. SEE HSU, THE GREAT DYING, 1986

17 QUOTED IN NATIONAL GEOGRAPHIC JUNE 1989 P 673

18 QUOTED IN SCIENTIFIC AMERICAN, DEC 1955 P37

19 "INSECTS IN AMBER" SCIENTIFIC AMERICAN NOV. 1951

20 DARWIN ALSO SAID "NATURUM NON FACIT SALTUM"-NATURE DOES NOT MAKE LEAPS. EVEN DURING HIS LIFETIME THIS BECAME UNTENABLE. IN HIS LATER WRITINGS DARWIN BACKED OFF, AND LET OTHER THEORIES OF EVOLUTION PLAY A SMALL PART.

Notes to part three

1 INT J CANCER 1991 49:208-93

2 AM J EPIDEMIOLOGY 1992 SEP 15:136(6) : 686-97

3 N ENG J MED 1991 JUN 27:324 (26) :1839-44

4 A WIDELY PUBLICIZED REPORT IN THE *NEW ENGLAND JOURNAL OF MEDICINE* SEPTEMBER 14, 1995, CONCLUDED THAT THE LOWEST MORTALITY WAS OBSERVED IN WOMEN AT LEAST 15% BELOW THE U.S. AVERAGE WEIGHT. THE ACTUAL DATA IN THE REPORT, HOWEVER, SHOWED THAT MORTALITY WAS LOWER FOR WOMEN WHO WERE AS MUCH AS 50% OVER THE "OPTIMAL" WEIGHT. TO OBTAIN THE RESULTS THAT THE RESEARCHER REPORTED, LESS THAN 32% OF THE ACTUAL RECORDED DEATHS WAS INCLUDED (1,499 OUT OF 4,726 DEATHS). EVEN IF THE SELECTION USED BY THE RESEARCHERS IS VALID, IT DOES NOT APPLY TO ALMOST 70% OF THE POPULATION.

ANOTHER ARTICLE IN THE SAME ISSUE WAS WIDELY REPORTED TO SHOW NO INCREASED MORTALITY FROM WEIGHT LOSS. THE REPORT, HOWEVER, INCLUDED MANY POINTS THAT CORROBORATE THE DANGERS OF WEIGHT LOSS. THE FOLLOWING IS A QUOTATION FROM THAT ARTICLE, "MEN LOSING MORE THAN 4.5 KG HAD, INDEPENDENTLY OF THE LEVEL OF WEIGHT AT THE BASELINE AND THE CONFOUNDERS, A *SIGNIFICANTLY ELEVATED RISK OF DEATH* FROM NONCARDIOVASCULAR AND NONCANCEROUS CAUSES *AND FROM ALL CAUSES*" (ITALICS MINE). THE STUDY ALSO FOUND THAT "THE SUBJECTS WHOSE WEIGHT FLUCTUATED THE MOST HAD A SIGNIFICANTLY HIGHER RISK OF DEATH...." THE CONCLUSIONS REPORTED IN THE PRESS THAT WEIGHT LOSS WAS NOT ASSOCIATED WITH HIGHER MORTALITY RELATED ONLY TO A SMALL GROUP OF MEN THAT HAD NONE OF THE COMMON RISK FACTORS FOUND IN THE GENERAL POPULATION. THIS STUDY, AS ALMOST ALL STUDIES, FOUND MEN IN GENERAL, WHO LOST WEIGHT, FACED AN INCREASE IN MORTALITY.

5 THE DISASTER LOBBY, MELVIN GRAYSON, THOMAS SHEPARD, FOLLETT PUBLISHING 1973

6 AMERICAN HEALTH MAGAZINE JUNE 1990 VOL IX NO 5 P 44FF

7 JAMA 1975 231:360-381

8 CIRCULATION VOL 82 NO 6 DEC 1990 P 1916

9 FOOD AND HEALING, NEW YORK: BALLENTINE BOOKS, 1986

10 ANIMAL TESTS ARE NOT PERFECT SURROGATE TESTS FOR HUMAN BEINGS. ANOTHER SAFE DRUG THAT IS DEADLY TO AN ANIMAL IS ACETOMINOPHEN (TYLONOL) WHICH CAN CAUSE SERIOUS HARM TO CATS

11 INSIGHT, NOV 5, 1990 P57

Notes to part four

1 ENCYCLOPEDIA AMERICANA

2 CATHOLIC ENCYCLOPEDIA

3 J.G.FRAZER, THE GOLDEN BOUGH P.345

Notes to part five

1 ACCIDENT FACTS 1989 EDITION, NATIONAL SAFETY COUNCIL P57

2 ACCIDENT FACTS 1988 EDITION NATIONAL SAFETY COUNCIL PG 65

3 ACCIDENT FACTS 1989 EDITION NATIONAL SAFETY COUNCIL PG 65

4 IBID

5 IBID

6 IBID

7 US NEWS AND WORLD REPORTS 8-15-88

8 IBID

9 OP CIT

10 SPEED VARIANCE AND ITS INFLUENCE ON ACCIDENTS   N J GARBER, R GADIRAU JULY 1988

11 IBID

12 IBID

13 ALASKA, LAST AMERICAN FRONTIER, MERLE COLBY MACMILLAN AND CO 1939

14 PHILA. INQUIRER MAY 22, 1993

B

C

144

D

146

EVOLUTION OF FLYING INSECTS, 82
EVOLUTIONISTS, 84
EXCRETORY SYSTEM, 112
EXECUTIVE COMMITTEE OF THE SOVIET, 38
EXTINCTION, 81- 83
EYE, 83

F

I

149

J

K

L

M

N

O

P

Q

R

S

SHEEP, 79
SIENNA, 16
SILENT SPRING, 91
SIN, 113
SINGAPORE, 35
SIOUX, 50
SIR HUMPHRY DAVY, 21
SIR OLIVER LODGE, 27
SIR WILLIAM CROOKES, 21
SKULL, 48
SLASH AND BURN LOGGING, 54
SLEEPING BEAUTY, 126
SOCIALISTS, 38
SOLANINE, 92
SOLAR SYSTEM, 67
SOLOMON, 109
SONAR LIKE ADAPTATION, 74
SOUIX WAR OF 1876, 50
SOUL, 108, 109
SOVIET, 40
SOVIET UNION, 12
SPEED LIMIT, 118-122
SPEED VARIANCE, 121
SPIDER, 82
SPIN DOCTORS, 69
SPINERET AND WEB, 82
SPOTS ON THE SUN, 16
SRI LANKA, 104
ST PATRICK, 131
ST. PETERSBURG DOCKYARDS, 21
ST.VALENTINE'S DAY, 115
STAPHYLOCOCCI, STREPTOCOCCI, THE BACILLI
   OF DIPTHERIA, AND ANTHRAX, 100
STARS, 68
STATES, 118
STATISTICAL ABSTRACT, 135
STINGING POLYP, 78
STOCKBROKER, 25
STOCKBROKER INTRODUCED TESLA, 25
STONE OF SCONE, 12
STOP PRISON RAPE, 136
STRIKERS, 37
STRIKERS TRIED TO PROSELYTIZE THE TROOPS, 38
STRONG NUCLEAR FORCE, 56
STRONG, BENJAMIN, 44
SUB SEA VOLCANO, 65
SUB-CLINICAL DISEASES, 89
SUDDEN ACCELERATION, 105
SUFANILAMIDE, 100

Y

Order Form

To order additional copies of "Things You Know That Are Not So".

For charge card orders call 1-800-266-5564.

Mail order: Russet Press, P.O. Box 854, Voorhees NJ 08043

Name:_____

Address:_____

City:_____State:_____Zip:_____

Telephone: (_____)_____

Send $12.95 plus $3.00 for shipping. Please allow 3-4 weeks for delivery.

Add 6% sales tax for books shipped to a New Jersey address.